How to Homeschool

A Guide for Progressive Parents

MIGUEL VARELLA-CID

How to Homeschool: A Guide for Progressive Parents

First published in 2022 by

Panoma Press Ltd
a Rethink Press company
www.rethinkpress.com
www.panomapress.com

Book layout by Neil Coe.
Research Editor: Carlos Queiros.

978-1-784529-65-9

The right of Miguel Varella-Cid to be identified as the author of this work has been asserted in accordance with sections 77 and 78 of the Copyright, Designs and Patents Act 1988.

A CIP catalogue record for this book is available from the British Library.

This book is available online and in bookstores.

Acknowledgement

To Yuko, Arina, Akira, and Mark – for sharing the greatest wealth of life.

Contents

Contents

INTRODUCTION

Writing this book was something I contemplated for a good number of years but didn't commit to fully until I felt a burning desire to share and make a difference that I could no longer contain nor postpone.

With all the deep responsibilities we take on as parents, and an awareness of a need to protect the children and nurture them with strong values and knowledge of the future we are living into, when ours came into this world, Yuko and I made the conscious choice to be unflinchingly truthful with each of them, and of course with one another.

Although, as almost every homeschool parent, we began with no personal experience, we set out with total commitment and faith we could offer each child a far more nurturing, empowering and inspirational form of learning and freedom through homeschooling. Little did we realize then just how much we'd learn and develop together as a family, and how well our children would naturally learn.

We chose to confront and question our own instilled fears and insecurities related to failure. We gave each child the choice to learn at home—if and when they'd become committed to homeschool options, or not...

Together, as a homeschooling family, we've practically explored the pros and cons of homeschooling. There are many names for it: Homeschooling, Unschooling, Free Schooling, to name a few. How our children learn shouldn't be a label; it is a unique process for each child, to be absorbed as and when the best time and opportunities present themselves.

We witnessed our daughter Arina's incredible homeschooling progress unfold, day by day, year by year. Today, we see how she has used her passion and inspiration for learning since the start of her life, and how she has become an amazingly talented, wise, courageous and capable young lady.

It took initially watching and embracing our younger son Akira's discoveries as an excitable but talented and budding engineer. It took learning for ourselves to overcome our fears and instead have faith in his playfulness and affinity for fun. It took me having faith in Yuko's naturally gentle attitude, patience, and wisdom to make the right choices as a great and natural mama. We know the best ways to influence them is the simplest: it is by example.

Would you agree that boredom and monotony typically fail to inspire, but can have opposite detrimental effects? Such negative traits, if imposed regularly, carry the danger of quashing a child's natural inquisitiveness and passion for discovery.

In this book I will share how to form **homeschooling schedules and curriculums that work for your child.**

Homeschooling is a journey on which, traveling together, we cannot possibly fail. Your daughter already has much of what it takes when she is born. The main ingredients you can bring are being committed to their learning freedom and to love them.

A free homeschooling family is able and willing not to be forceful. Because through force and coercion, we are increasingly likely to invite reciprocating resistance, and possibly worse. We are willing to learn to be the best parents we can. Parents that our children will be thankful for and love sharing time with, growing together.

In each of their lasting interests, our goal is to facilitate and inspire, while sharing and discussing modern dangers they may want to avoid, and help the children to honestly navigate the reasons why.

Today's growing young person's addictions to smartphones, tablets, movies, and games is alarming, if not frightening.

The consequences visibly developing in children and young adults surround us in day-to-day life. Many don't understand yet, but they are the victims. Our children will observe and also come to realize:

Smartphones make us stupid.
Books make us smart.

Using homeschooling examples, we practically illustrate, so you'll in turn embrace early development of choice. Listen to, discuss, and exchange your thoughts, so your child becomes articulate. Choice, where there is no danger, is something we embraced from the very beginning for our family. Choice comes from the most powerful resolve and something we encourage parents to bestow on their children as early as possible, even when they first begin free homeschooling.

We instill human life-values through an environment of love, forthrightness, and encouragement, entangled with the inevitable temporary downfalls to be encountered on the natural paths of failure.

Mistakes are the process of discovering the direction for better results. Falling out of trees and bearing scrapes and small wounds strengthens their resolve.

For times of future challenges, failure instills bravery, due caution, and wisdom in a child's character, if not a practical understanding of basic physics.

Of course, homeschooled children benefit greatly from learning and understanding subjects such as sciences and mathematics, but they foster the practice of such subjects directly from experience. While concentrating on projects, math, science skills and knowledge can be absorbed and understood, where children often don't even realize. In making a small simple building from wood, for example, your daughter learns the practical use of arithmetic and trigonometry.

Together, we will explore how a deep understanding of academic subjects can be imbued with alacrity, so your child's learning is a natural joy, rather than being memorized classroom style, only later to be forgotten.

In harmony with Japanese culture, we encourage and immerse our children in situations where they may gain compassion and the consideration of others.

With the essential ingredients of homeschooling freedom and delight, children naturally develop their characters with the great qualities of passion for knowledge and a healthy curiosity for discovery.

In turn, as their self-belief becomes naturally widened and deeper, your children will thereby develop as adults who look forward to their amazing journeys and continued learning through life—where learning itself is naturally enjoyable.

The above is a glimpse of the homeschooling wealth that is available through free homeschooling.

Perhaps alarmingly for some, the examples I have given are ever less absorbed in modern school environments and learning.

Contemplation is to pierce illusion and experience reality.

Have you ever contemplated not only the importance of the part young people play in not only being our children but of their future as parents of our grandchildren and beyond?

We might consider ourselves challenged to be living in times of great challenge and possible change:

The Covid-19 pandemic is a grave threat.

The grave environmental challenges facing humanity and all life on earth too are solemn and unique.

The erosion of human rights we may face if humanity doesn't awake in time is also unprecedented.

Someday, how will each child become the remembered elders of their grandchildren's grandchildren amidst how much the world will probably change between now and then? What difference will they make in their lifetimes?

Planting seeds for the learning and enjoyment of others could well be one of our greatest responsibilities as we progress through life.

We are free to scatter seeds abundantly, some of which may only blossom when we are gone, but blossom they may if we nurture natural learning and growth.

Is it better to explore the power of the sea in safety, or let our children mindlessly surf the internet?

It is our choice to see the challenges of life today as positive opportunities and to actively seek and share the truth with all children, so they too may contemplate how to put right what continues to decline within the world we all share.

Will we choose to allow our children to be taught to be fearful of the future, as they stare mindlessly at screens and learn history written by the victors of wars as it is taught in schools, or will we share evenings looking at the night sky, huddled in deep in conversation, encouraging deeper knowledge and understanding?

In How to Homeschool, we together explore the natural ways humanity may collectively heal the earth—and for youngsters, share why the answer might not be found in aspiring to be driven by AI in electric cars, but instead in navigating to rediscover the pearls of wisdom of returning to natural farming, and focusing on living in harmony with nature, and not in spite of it. Through being in harmony with nature, we can organically return carbon to the earth and thereby reclaim it from Earth's atmosphere.

Nature teaches quiet wisdom, as the wind whispers through the trees and through life which our children can observe naturally and at their own pace, and this is one of many reasons why we encourage exploring it.

Schools today seldom contemplate and leave children with questions about such essentials for humanity's continued existence. Instead, it is our observation they increasingly tend to encourage children to memorize and regurgitate "facts" without questioning them.

If such is truly the case, today's schoolchildren may be widely missing opportunities to learn to think critically. Critical thinking is one essence of natural and free homeschooling.

When we focus on the possibilities of free homeschooling and learning, we give youngsters the chance to correct the mistakes our generations have made.

Children are the inspiring farmers, innovators, inventors, authors, artists, creators, healers, teachers, and leaders of their future. They must be in lockstep with all of humanity's growth and our return to nature, and not in competition with it.

We believe for a successful future existence we must better equip as many children as possible. Not through force, but in consciously inspired ways, where love is our most powerful strength of all, where:

Love is the acceptance of another without condition.

In this book, we share many examples to instill an understanding of how to encourage your child's self-development and motivation, so your homeschooled children naturally build the drive and desire for progress, as adults for the better combined good where they will face life's challenging endeavors.

Learning and study has always been a natural part of natural life, not just in the classroom. You will understand how each child is different and unique in their ways of learning, and how to recognize your son's strengths.

You will understand the empowerment and importance of encouraging your child to develop social skills. Not just with children of similar age, but people of all ages and many walks of life. Shyness isn't a condition; it is often an unconscious choice that is avoidable.

You'll learn how to recognize their individual qualities and traits too, so you and the community you create together with others can help develop your daughter's unique homeschool talents and interests.

We share how to deal with other pitfalls of homeschooling and how to get through the tougher days, which will challenge but not overcome you.

We describe the typical mistakes parents make when starting out homeschooling, and perhaps more importantly, why, if left unchecked, these can lead to undesirable habits and can reduce children's progress.

We share how to recognize the dangers of inexperience and how to empower your child's learning and grace. You'll thereby become empowered in how to avoid instilling fears of failure and uncertainty, to instead help your daughter become confident of her choices and development.

If your children are attending school and your family want to try homeschooling, you don't have to wait. Homeschooling Wealth is possible to develop, even while your kids are still attending state schools. What we offer works during your child's free time, as not least in the many different ways of learning that are possible, often they don't even realize they are learning because they're having fun!

This book is not only for parents and relatives considering a complete homeschooling future for their child, but even for those considering something in between. There is no homeschool curriculum that states homeschooling must be for a child's entire education. Homeschooling can be for as long as your child is inspired.

The freedom is there for your child and you to tailor learning toward the affinity for the subjects he chooses to concentrate attention and energies on. The choices are boundless in free homeschooling.

We feel empathy for the many families who may have a strong desire, but feel they don't have the luxury of choice in offering their children homeschooling.

We each make choices from perceived realities and we must not only understand these perceived realities and how they affect us (positively or negatively), but realize and instill the immense power of choice within our children, rather than impose limits, where possible.

The will to overcome our fears and to foster the gumption to be unstoppable in the goals we feel are important is where the wealth of life is to be found for each of us as individuals.

Some completely miss the possibilities and believe they just don't have the choice or luxury. Some may, without looking into it, convince themselves before they even begin that they cannot afford the expense of homeschooling.

From many parents we've seen find their homeschooling success stories against the odds, we would gently encourage due consideration of How to Homeschool before making your decision.

In these unprecedented pandemic times, especially for so many more now than ever before, the opportunity and time for many parents to embrace homeschooling their children in entirety, or the hybridization of home and conventional schooling, has truly come of age.

It is our intent How to Homeschool will continue growing its community, which can in time follow a momentum of its own, through the committed parents we will doubtlessly meet and build rich relationships with. Our intention as we expand resources is to share inspiring homeschooling content with you. There is wealth to be gleaned from literary art, and much, much more.

In becoming a reader of How to Homeschool, we warmly invite you to join our free homeschool mailing list.

You and your children will not only become lifetime community members, and receive the free bonus chapter listed in Contents, but continuously receive updates on the effective wisdom of natural learning as we grow.

For FREE!

Subscribe: howtohomeschool.life

Would you like to explore the unforgettable journey of learning together with children, and watch them blossom in beautiful ways you cannot yet imagine? Does the notion of continuing to build a unique relationship together that will become a core of their adult lives sound appealing?

Do you truly want to give your child the best possible chance of a fulfilled life?

Yes? Great!

Let's begin.

WE BECOME WHAT WE BELIEVE WE ARE

___

1 We Are The Product Of Our Past

First off, I'd like to warmly acknowledge you for taking steps to research what free homeschooling offers.

In unprecedented times, where conventional children's school education has been so negatively affected and is likely to be further worsened in years to come, I am certain that many parents must be concerned, and rightly so, for their child's future.

Children have grown depressed, in record numbers. Some have become afraid of close contact with others, and many have seen their parents suffer terribly, whether from financial difficulties, or loss of relationships with others.

It's been a terrible time for countless people, and some will have felt a deep sense of hopelessness, even despair at times.

I know Yuko and I would have felt much of the above if we hadn't discovered the empowerment that free homeschooling offers in the development of our children and others we have delighted in watching develop.

I want to say, from the outset, Yuko and I are committed to sharing with you the immense wealth that comes from free homeschooling that we have deeply explored. In my case, as a thinker who learns primarily from observation, some of my sharing comes from my own experiences as a child, right the way to being over 50 years old.

Yuko consistently puts me in awe of her natural wisdom to be a great mother, and much of what I share is from seeing children learn naturally through her eyes.

Truth is, in recent times of lockdowns, social distancing and conventional schooling culminating in many children staying at home need not be the erosion of children's education, but instead a conscious opportunity for their vast improvement in learning, and beyond.

Yes, now more than ever we have the freedom to vastly improve children's learning and skills, coming from a place of love, inspiration, wonder, and excitement.

Free homeschooling offers education that allows them to become adults who will have spent a childhood developing their unique talents. Their acquired skills will enable them to naturally progress on to doing what makes them happy. As happy individuals, children naturally grow into self-confident people who know what they want, and don't feel they need to be given permission to progress in life.

We have seen how countless parents around the world, who have put all their faith in conventional schooling, see the erosion, but not having explored other options can be at a loss for what to do. This is what inspired me to write this book. Our vision is to make as big a difference for humanity as we possibly can, where the "Why?" is infinitely bigger than we are, and through sharing of our triumphs and challenges, we can illustrate the "How" of free homeschooling.

We are unflinchingly committed to generously contributing our lives to helping you and your children achieve true greatness in the face of challenge. Although it's unlikely we'll share the same story, I hope yours might resonate.

Let's go back some 40+ years, to start at the very beginning, so in turn, you'll be able to understand why we chose to homeschool in the first place, and how we came to immerse our own children in freedom to learn from passion: free homeschooling.

My own childhood included a school education with unusual and interesting twists along the way, from which in turn I took observations and experiences that have served well in my understanding of self-motivated learning.

In contrast, Yuko was entirely educated through Japanese state schools, on a smaller island of Japan, in deep countryside, surrounded by nature and beautiful ocean. She too was an ardent learner and not least, clearly enriched and endowed with wisdom through being immersed in a natural, slower pace of life and a close family.

Despite our childhoods having been spent in entirely different cultures, the instilled result is that, in each of us, a deep desire grew to want to bring up our future children in the countryside. Yuko had always dreamt of living in a forest and I had never quite understood the logic of people wanting to live in large cities, when there is so much more to be gained and enjoyed from living in natural surroundings.

I was born and mostly brought up in the UK, although through my parents' course of life together, I spent my kindergarten years first in Mozambique, then Portugal, where I learned my first language. By the time we returned to the UK when I was five, I had forgotten my first English words learned before we moved to Africa.

Within weeks I had again learned to speak basic English, through being dropped into the melting pot of life at a local public primary school, across the road from our home in West London.

I remember one thing from the school assemblies, which has always stayed with me and I still value as my own value to this day. In unity, every day we children would recite:

"Only my best is good enough for me."

I had to play catch-up with my reading abilities through having extra after-school classes (the first taste of homeschooling-I experienced). Despite being slow to start with, by the age of eight I'd developed an interest in reading children's adventure stories by Enid Blyton and progressed rapidly from there. I can thank my mother and tutor for instinctively knowing which seeds to plant for me.

Through my father's work, I developed a natural interest in cars at a very early stage, and once I could read, I'd regularly visit the local newsagents store, ravenously reading every car magazine cover to cover. I'd get numb legs from being crouched down there for hours, but wouldn't even realize it until I tried to get up and walk.

My preferred choice became a particularly well-written glossy car publication that had better pictures and writing eloquence. I was so engrossed in learning every piece of information about beautiful cars, I didn't realize the many other important benefits I was absorbing. Little did I realize my interest and hobby would, in turn, go on to serve me well for my chosen future.

At the age of 11, I was sent off to a boarding school, with fees generously paid by my local education authority. Aside from enjoying much time outdoors, playing in the forest and fishing for trout, I was taught little of any academic education to speak of.

But learn I certainly did. I continued to read, because I had a passion for the content I chose to immerse myself in and gain pleasure from. I also learned plenty of basic woodworking and pottery. I continued to improve and made ever finer pieces.

At 13, I realized I wasn't really being challenged and felt that, academically, I had a desire to learn more. I distinctly remember my teacher comparing me to another boy, saying he'd make something of himself someday, but he didn't hold out much hope for me. This didn't discourage me, but instead had the opposite effect. Perhaps this had been the intention? I may never know.

That year, at the annual review by my local education authority, I politely requested that I be moved to somewhere I could get an education that would enable me to attend university in future. I was fortunate that the three little old ladies who'd visit once a year to appraise my progress took my request most seriously.

My request led to being offered a place at the other end of the spectrum, into what would in turn become my best educational years. To this day I am deeply thankful for their kindness. Their resolve helped me learn and form some of the content I share within this book.

I was transferred to St. Christopher School, Letchworth, England—a liberal, co-ed boarding school with a focus on self-government, with children ranging from others like myself who were from poorer families, or who had no parents at all, to the opposite end of the spectrum: children of wealthy, successful families from all over the world.

At St. Chris there was no significant distinction between those who were from wealthy backgrounds and those who weren't. We were essentially equal and opportunities to become elected officials were based on personal merit. All teachers including the headmaster were addressed only by their first names. There was no physical punishment, although some of the teachers would shout at the children.

St. Chris was a vegetarian school offering excellent facilities and teaching, with a focus on provision of choices, where possible. There was a wide range of outdoor activities, which included such choices as mountain climbing, skiing, camping and sailing.

I mentioned self-government. We'd have weekly school council meetings. Everybody was welcome to attend, and we'd discuss everything we felt was of importance. Proposed motions would be put to the vote in meetings held in the theater building.

Many people's greatest fear is to speak in front of large crowds.

Thus, students had the opportunity to choose to speak in public, and thereby would soon lose the fear of presenting their ideas to large groups. This is especially empowering for children when discussing something they may be passionate about.

I recall having been very afraid of getting up and risking making a fool of myself as a teenager, but then later I came to the realization that an audience isn't there to judge us, but that people are willing to consider, absorb, and even support what it is we rise to share.

I was placed in all of the lower level classes of my year for the first term I attended, so I could catch up on subjects. By the second term, with the school having seen just how committed I was, and the fast progress I made as a result, I was transferred to all of the top classes where I continued ravenously to study and absorb knowledge.

Ultimately, having started with virtually nothing, I ended up with 13 O-Levels, all at high grades, within just two-and-a-half years. I had in that short space of time not only caught up with most of my classmates, but overtaken most of them through my sheer desire for achievement and learning.

I share this story to illustrate how fast homeschoolers can learn if they embrace the empowerment of self-commitment, which in turn is most naturally absorbed through activities they most enjoy.

We have learned that there is no need to rush our children to absorb knowledge in fear they may be left behind. We must practice patience, and inspire them to learn through curiosity, mystery, and positive forms of self-motivational encouragement, and last, but perhaps most importantly, love.

Having looked deeply into my past, I realize my motivations weren't necessarily the healthiest, despite seemingly excellent exam results. I became a person who was competitive and self-driven, but my major drive factor was borne from fear of failure (such as tests and exams). Should this not be avoided in a child's education, or part of conventional schooling?

Fear, whilst it keeps us safe where there may be danger, can also be debilitating, as some of us who look deeper later may come to the realization of, for ourselves. Fear is often what stops us from making great strides in life, and can ultimately stop us living our dreams into reality and beyond.

Had I not come to recognize and confront my fear of failure (through self-development learning with an empowering organization called Landmark Worldwide), just before I turned 30, I know now I would not have moved to Japan, to continue my journey with nothing but a suitcase containing only essential clothes.

Despite my instilled fear of failure, I arrived in Tokyo with only a dream and a will to create a life I'd love. In the subsequent 20 years I have gone on to create the life we are inspired by, having met Yuko four years after arriving. Together, we continue to learn and expand, knowing full well that if we are not growing and contributing to others, we are doing the opposite: slowly dying.

Being a person who learns mostly from observation (each of us has a particular sense from which we tend to learn best. I will discuss this later, in Homeschooling Resources), I observed that many of my school colleagues didn't share my interest in sciences, but instead had better aptitude for other things such as theater and music. They were encouraged by our unique school to develop in those directions, rather than being coerced into repetition of what they had no interest in.

Still in touch with some of my classmates today, I see that those who followed through with their interests, as I also did, have gone on to live lives they enjoy. They're not necessarily financially wealthy, but wealthy in the relationships they are surrounded by. **The quality of our lives is given by the relationships we create around us, which is indeed the greatest wealth of all. It is in turn through relationships that we in turn create prosperity.**

At St. Chris, I also made teenage friends who arrived from Asia with no English language ability. Amazingly, within months, I observed they could hold a basic conversation and follow science classes taught in full English. Their English often became fluent within a year, which may seem remarkable, especially as their abilities mostly developed through after-school conversations.

Little did I know that some of these experiences and observations would someday help and encourage me to understand and have greater faith in children's abilities, especially in the context of free homeschooling.

I went on to study at university, where through a fortunate accident, I ended up not doing what I'd applied for and, through fear of failure, had come to believe I wanted to do.

My vision had been to study dentistry, but in all honesty, this was because I had believed it was the way to become wealthy and achieve the materially privileged life I'd seen of my father's Harley Street dentist friend's life. I too wanted his lifestyle, but knew I didn't really have an interest in looking inside people's often smelly mouths and working on their teeth.

Instead, I changed to study something related to my first passion—mechanical engineering. Unfortunately, the course turned out to be mostly theoretical and devoid of almost all practical aspects. I was bored by non-interactive lectures and would find my mind wandering. Sometimes, I mulled that I would have been better off studying law, or business, but today I realize it was all a part of my journey, which I want to share the fruits of in turn to help others.

Through confronting my fear of failure, I put myself on a path to the future I wanted most: I wanted to be happy.

My happiness in turn became possible through the ability to create relationships.

I vividly recall when I was 15. Interrupting my intense concentration on homework, one of my teachers with 30+ years of experience who'd seen countless children develop and observed their progress through life, sat beside me with a smile and asked, "Miguel, what do you think is the most important—academic studies, or the development of social skills?"

I replied, "The former." He replied, "No, it's social development." I was surprised and sat there contemplating why he'd said that. Years later, I came to realize John was a great teacher. Not only did he say something I have never forgotten, but that afternoon, he left me with more questions than I had before he spoke with me. I have also come to realize, through life experience and observations, that he was absolutely right.

I made possible the future I wanted by contacting the Japanese company I really wanted a job with, and offering the CEO my services for free, to prove my worth. All I asked for was a desk and a telephone, to prove my worth inside a week. I promised him that if after that week he didn't want to hire me, I'd go, and he'd owe me nothing.

I was offered the position I had wanted, after just four days, and went on to increase their international business by 30% in the first year. This, and much more, became possible through learning to authentically build what John had suggested: relationships with others.

Through time, despite our age differences, I couldn't help but notice that each of my three younger brothers also developed into working with what they individually had a strong interest in as children.

Today, we each have a passion for what we do, and being excellent at our work have each gone on to create success and recognition in our chosen professions. See, our choices were ours to make. We weren't coerced into our vocations by our parents or teachers. In my case, my father had me help out at his workshop. I was largely left to my own devices, to tinker and play, and so a love for mechanical things grew naturally.

Boarding schools located in English countryside brought me into daily contact with nature. At the first school, I would build dams in small streams with my friends. We'd go fishing, climb trees and play in the forest. Then as I got older, at St. Christopher School, I took up sailing, windsurfing, hiking, camping, and rock-climbing. These experiences would first instill a basic understanding of the grounding that access to nature can bring, and would develop from there.

I learned about the importance of fellowship. On occasion, I would be invited to spend weekends away from boarding school, and later with my university classmates, in their homes. I am thankful for having been warmly welcomed into some of my friends' families, and to this day feel very fortunate to have experienced genuine family intimacy of spending time with friends, while naturally also getting to know their inspiring parents.

My keen sense of learning from observation helped me to absorb what were the particularly beneficial aspects of good family life. For example, I recall being inspired at how one American family would encourage particularly engaging conversations over lunch, or the empowerment that a friend's mother's care, with whom I am still friends today, provided for me as a child. I felt a great kindness from such welcoming families who treated me as one of their own.

How these people made me feel is the reason I will never forget them.

I met Yuko in 2002 and realized in 2005 that despite my fears of marrying the wrong lady and making the mistake my parents had, I couldn't possibly imagine a life without her.

I'll share more later about the importance of a strong parental connection for our children. I'd like to generously acknowledge Yuko as my core strength and the why she is the glue that keeps together the strongest family bond between us.

She gives of herself selflessly and generously, each and every day, so our family relationships, interconnectivity and understanding of one another continuously expands. I am constantly inspired by her unflinching commitment and the beauty of how she conducts herself, so gently inspires us. She is an old soul, gracefully carrying a wisdom accumulated from many lives and I love her for all she is. I am here to serve, love, and learn from her, and make sure she is always well cared for.

As parents do, we often discuss our children during our free time alone, but without doubt, were it not for her commitment, we wouldn't have found the success in homeschooling our children that we are enjoying today.

Yuko was brought up on a small island of Japan about three hours' boat ride off the coast of Kobe. Shodoshima is a peaceful island with a population of around 30,000. She walked to and swam in the ocean most days of the warmer months, and played outdoors with her two brothers. She was an excellent, dedicated student who consistently scored high marks right through her schooling years. Being Japanese, she was taught to comply with rules, in the typical manner in which students are taught in Japan.

Her father worked hard to provide for his wife and three children, but Yuko was mostly brought up by her mother and grandmother in a conventional Japanese way, with a traditional countryside flavor of life.

When she was 17, Yuko left the island and went to study at college in Kobe for a couple of years, before starting her career.

Following the great Kobe earthquake, she moved to Tokyo as work opportunities presented themselves.

She discovered international travel during her 20s. She spent three years in the UK to learn English, before spending six months in India traveling by herself, after which she returned to Japan. She thereafter continued work for three months at a time to afford travel to Southeast Asian countries and to the Middle East to explore and sample life and culture there, for months at a time, usually traveling alone in Third World countries.

It was through her travels and observations of life while meeting and befriending the local people that she began to gain an understanding that not all people around the world are schooled in the same way as she had been in Japan. This difference in daily family lives in other far-flung countries helped grow her curiosity about different cultures. The differences in their ways of being were clear, as being the product of their pasts.

Similarly, you as a parent are a product of your past, as is your partner. It may serve each of us to really look back at our past. In doing so, some of us may see the many poignant times that would have left a mark on each of us. I myself cannot forget being bullied (in the first boarding school), and I have also come to learn that such difficulties are able to teach us more and make us stronger, so that we can be better prepared for the life ahead we want to create.

For example, from my experiences of being treated in a cruel manner, I learned to have compassion for others, which in turn indirectly led me to writing this book. I want to share and provide knowledge I know other concerned parents may greatly appreciate when looking for the best solution for giving our children a brighter future.

With an understanding of relationships gleaned from our own childhoods, or if not, from others who are open and honest in their sharing of their experiences, we can gain an understanding of how our children, enrolled in conventional schooling, are (possibly negatively) affected in their current day-to-day lives.

Yuko and I have looked deeply at this, especially since our children were born, and whilst we refrain from being overly protective (and thereby perhaps stifling the freedom from which they may grow, in learning from their mistakes), we speak with them, and share our experiences and what we learned ourselves, while giving them as much freedom of choice as possible.

Our intention for each of our children is that they make as many choices as we can allow and facilitate, as they grow up (on the proviso that risks too big/dangers too great are avoided), so that they learn from a young age of the responsibilities they must take and become good at making important choices.

Our youngest learned, by the age of seven:

"A mistake is only a mistake when I refuse to correct it."

We believe that with homeschooling our children haven't suffered such negative experiences as being bullied, nor had many experiences of being told they're inept at a skill they're trying to learn; instead, they've been shown love and respect and been encouraged to explore and share their passions.

We've also mixed them with as many other children and adults of different walks of life as possible (more of this in The Myths of Homeschooling); from befriending other children in Third World countries during our travels and seeing how blessed we each are, to meeting and speaking directly with government ministers of Japan working in improvement of education.

What is clear is children who get to speak with many people, rather than being segregated into groups of the same age only, can develop a better ability to befriend anybody they meet, even while they are still young children.

2 When to Homeschool

I hope your story of what led you to the point of you first considering homeschooling for your child is as positive as our own which I'm about to share.

We are aware that although there are lots of happy stories, there are equally many which are not borne from happy situations, and we feel it's of great importance to help parents facing such challenges within this chapter.

Many of us parents are today being faced with seemingly insurmountable challenges that may lead to the inevitability of choosing homeschooling. It could be because our child is being bullied at school (or online), is depressed, has learning difficulties, detests Covid-19-related requirements, is simply not allowed to attend school because of government imposed social distancing, or any other myriad of differing circumstances, which results in his objection to attending conventional school, or learning online.

If you and your child(ren) find yourselves facing some of these challenges, please know our commitment is to help you as much as we can. What we have come to understand about children's natural learning, and beyond, is too valuable to not be shared as widely as possible in these unprecedented times.

Writing this book is a project that is much bigger than myself and my family. It is far bigger than a mere book. It is about you and countless others, and a possibility to together create a global movement in children's learning, where every child in whose lives we plant a seed can go on to grow and create their own experiences and enriched childhoods of natural learning.

Our possibility is that How to Homeschool will lead to the creation of a transformative, perpetually expanding, global online community with over 1,000,000 families, by January 1st, 2025.

This is how committed we are to endowing as many children as possible with a happiness and direction that continues to provide fulfillment and commitment to what they most want to achieve throughout their lives, which in turn will become self-perpetuating.

We intend to help you, not only through this book, but through podcasts, video courses, book lists and webinars we intend to begin creating, once we see this publication is reaching a sufficient number of people. The more people we can reach, the more proceeds we intend to reinvest in reaching more people, and we hope to help those most in need to access as much of what we have to share for free.

In this chapter about when to start homeschooling, I will share not just our own family experiences along the path to making the choice to do so, or not, but also the benefit of other people's more challenging choices, and the outcomes we've seen.

By looking at genuine stories of both happy and the most challenging of scenarios, where ultimately the right solution was found and how, we hope to cover an aspect that most helps your understanding of what choice may work best for you and your child. I may jump between our own story and other people's as a means with which to present contrasting scenarios.

Since the birth of our daughter Arina, the transformation of our lives was in no way unique. Parents will meet unimaginable challenges to support their family, and it's at times such as these that great strides are taken. That's how empowering love can be. Many parents choose to reject advice from others in such times, choosing instead to use their parental instincts, and they can make decisions that are borne from their own care, thoughts, and love.

Our daughter's early outdoor experiences were the beautiful countryside around Mount Fuji. First in her stroller, we'd walk our dog twice daily. Later, as she began to walk, we'd play in the parks, sometimes spend afternoons by a lakeside, and sometimes lay together by a lake under the bright moonlit sky, looking up at stars, with clouds rushing by above us as if in an outdoor planetarium.

In those days, although we were exploring and discussing possibilities, we still hadn't made any firm intentions to homeschool her, even though we had family and friends with vast experience they were willing to share of homeschooling large numbers of children together in a Christian community.

We'd witnessed their paths of progress, and the resultant fruits borne from their commitments to their children, the oldest of whom were at the time young adults about to emerge out into the world to find their own ways.

We visited other parents, both in Japan and other countries during our travels in our early years as a family, who'd also educated their children at home. A seed for the possibility to homeschool our own had been planted a long time ago and now it was up to us to let it blossom if we so chose.

Although Yuko and I are both believers in God, we have different interpretations in our faiths, and our intentions were not to indoctrinate beliefs into our children, but rather to give them the grace of time to choose for themselves, something which has naturally become a core flavor of the free homeschooling style we've adopted and continued to develop, in line with observing, sharing, and gaining understanding.

Finding success and happiness while living in the countryside has been a blessing I would warmly encourage others to explore if possible.

At first, Arina, when aged 18 months, joined a small new nursery for a few hours a day, as we felt it important for her to also mix with other children. She clearly didn't like to be away from Mama, but we continued, not least as it would give Yuko a much-needed break, so she could do other things she felt the need to, and have her own time.

I recall, as yet relatively inexperienced parents, nonetheless, we didn't approve that they used a TV to occupy the children's minds. The garden in which they played was not only very small, but quite unnatural, with only plastic toys, and grass sprayed with insecticides and herbicides.

Just after our daughter turned two, we found the home from where I sit writing this book today. The Lord blessed us in finding a 300-year-old traditional but solid Japanese farmhouse needing considerable cosmetic and modernization work, set in a sizable forest of 1.2 hectares.

While juggling running a business by day, in seemingly every spare waking hour, I worked hard with a talented friend for eight months to prepare our home, knowing that God had made this home possible, not just for our use, but for the benefit of others. This was too large just for a family of four, and I felt the Lord had other plans in store. There was a purpose within this blessing, and being entrusted with this piece of history, we would have freedom to in turn create history ourselves.

By this time, Yuko was heavily pregnant with our second child. Just as with our first, she wanted to have a natural birth, so I was racing against time. Just two months after we moved in, our new son Akira was born. Unlike his sister, who had stayed in the warmth and comfort of Mama's belly for as long as she could, Akira was energetic and couldn't wait to get out. It makes me smile to remember these clues hinted how today I would describe their characters in a nutshell.

Our children were each fortunate to be accepted to join a small but very natural kindergarten school (Asoubimura, which means "play-village"), offering no academic curriculum. A Steiner-styled facility for around 40 children, where, in turn, they each enjoyed three years cementing their first friendships.

The ethos of this school was based on play with other children, combined with an integration with nature and on-site naturally grown foods. Food was mostly prepared by the non-working mothers and they too had fun and would build community with one another.

At Asoubimura, there was no television, no plastic toys, nor any chemically treated outdoor environment. The children were encouraged to splash in muddy puddles, play in sand, climb trees, care for animals, be involved in handicrafts, and participate in everything from shearing sheep, planting vegetables, collecting eggs, through preparing foods, and playing—lots!

There was no academic learning whatsoever. Not even internet, although there was often music, usually live as the children practiced for plays, wearing costumes they made. Plenty of conversation, singing and dancing in coordination, and lots of laughter. It was interesting to know some of the parents, several of whom had spent three of their early years at Asoubimura as young children.

Yuko and I had both been passionate about travel and discovery even before we met, so it was a natural progression once together and with a young family to take our children abroad and, as much as possible, continue to explore, only together. We were practically aware from the outset that travel broadens the mind.

When our daughter was four-and-a-half and our son one-and-a-half, we took a month's trip to New Zealand's South Island, where I concentrated on completing a permaculture design course for two weeks. Yuko and the kids went on a road trip to explore the North Island, together with two adventurous friends who'd flown out with us—a Japanese mother and her young son.

This was to be the earliest trip which our daughter still has memories of, and to this day, she enjoys the memories as her earliest realization that there's a stunning world outside. Perhaps it was there that a seed was planted, which set off her love for nature and a serious commitment to preserve it.

In time, these experiences combined with others of seeing

immense natural beauty, or even visiting Third World countries, would pay off in ways we couldn't possibly imagine.

Arina continued to grow an interest in drawing, her skills improving in leaps and bounds by the time she was six. She'd loved hearing stories together with me at home, and had learned how to read basic English by the time she was of age to join the first year of Japanese public primary school.

Yuko and I were all too aware that conventional Japanese schooling is militaristic in its style and there is a focus on a lot of memorization.

Japanese are typically very disciplined, polite, and considerate of one another, but not as free to truly be themselves as they would likely benefit from, compared to, say, foreigners who didn't undergo Japanese schooling.

Not least, children are expected to know how to read and write Japanese, inclusive of Chinese derived characters, by the time they get to 12 years of age, which includes memorizing around 2,000 characters. To remember all of these, the teaching methods are predictably intensive.

Students of Japanese schools start at first year of primary with only 20 minutes of playtime and the amount of play progressively lessens, while school hours run longer with each progressive year, culminating in high school studying till the evening, followed by cram school after an early dinner, often taking their return to home way past 10:30 pm.

To me, from the onset, this militaristic way of teaching is a methodical way to train would-be salarymen who will work well in a rule-based work ethic. Quite the opposite of what I would see as a way to the inspired learning and development such as that I'd experienced during my own childhood.

I'd often ask myself why, especially in the world we find ourselves increasingly living in, where jobs are in rapid decline, with more and more daily work activities being replaced by AI, what sort of future are many children living into?

Perhaps not unlike yourself at this stage, our concerns were growing with some urgency to choose. Yuko started telling the staff and some of the mothers at Asoubimura that we were seriously considering homeschooling, before Arina was enrolled in primary school.

We were surprised to find that even the headmistress was very strongly against the idea, despite having decades of experience in having seen small children spend three years at her school and become adults who she continued to be in touch with. Some ex-students even put their own children in the same Asoubimura kindergarten, having a personal understanding of the great benefits to be gleaned from learning through play. What did they know that we didn't yet, I wondered?

Although we were more interested in homeschooling her than not, we ultimately decided we'd take a leap of faith and let our daughter choose for herself. Choice can be incredibly self-empowering, as discussed at the end of the last chapter.

So, at the end of her second year of school, Arina vehemently made the choice that she wanted to study at home. We facilitated this with all the encouragement, time, and materials we felt would support her choice, as well as finding a community of like-minded parents and children from whom we could learn and also share what we already knew, which might be of help to them. From having done that permaculture course in New Zealand, Yuko and I had come to understand that resilience and strength comes from being in community with one another.

One day, some time later, while hosting a gathering of homeschooling children at our home, Yuko was sitting around our kitchen table with the other mothers, where each was sharing her story of circumstances leading to their start of homeschooling.

At one point, she stopped and realized she was hearing a lot of stories of difficulties, struggle, and despair, quite different from our own family's experiences. Here were mothers in tears who shared harrowing stories of how their children had physically hurt themselves, in not wanting to attend school anymore because of bullying, or how their teachers had made them feel so small and incapable.

Some of their children had insisted so strongly, a few had suggested or even attempted to slit their wrists while still in primary school. Often their children, especially if young, would be unable to say in words why they so strongly demonstrated they didn't want to go to school, but they couldn't hide it in their demeanor and actions.

Many of these mothers' choices to begin homeschooling were desperate reactions to severely negative situations. Thankfully, in every case, Yuko was now sitting around our kitchen table surrounded by deeply caring mothers whose hindsight clearly showed they'd absolutely made the right choices to make homeschooling possible. They now each had the benefit of having seen the return of delight and happiness within their children's eyes, and their resolve was strengthened by it.

It still saddened some to see how affected they'd been in confusing and prioritizing what others would think over their children's desperation. Some of the mothers shared how free homeschooling was seen negatively by so many, including their relatives who had no experience of what free homeschooling was about. All they'd envisaged at first was that the child was to become a failure in society if not attending conventional school, which had made the decision all the more difficult for these mothers to ultimately choose to follow.

For some, they shared how their husbands hadn't agreed to homeschool their child to begin with, although in each case they'd managed to persuade them in the end, not least through their child's absolute refusal to attend school, and sometimes severe acts of desperation. Similarly, there were also some single mothers who had come to feel they had no choice but to offer what they felt could work, ultimately.

These were the stories that brought tears of sadness and compassion that day, as mothers remembered the mistakes they'd started out making in insisting their children attend. They had each been held back by fears of failure, while risking the damage that might result in forcing their child to attend, without realizing it.

Ultimately though, these mamas had all chosen to become peaceful fighters through having focused on lovingly and fully accepting their children, supporting their choices, and learning that it didn't matter what neighbors, friends, and family might have thought. The most important was their child, who did have the courage and conviction to say "no."

Some parents come to realize later that they pushed for too

long, which led to their children's further drop into a rabbit hole of negativity. In the more extreme cases that we know of, the child stopped all communication with anybody outside their home, because of their discomfort with being forced to attend school or be with people that they felt uncomfortable around.

We have observed on occasion the more children are forced to do something they are vehemently against, the more they will reject and be repelled by this forcefulness. We can expect that it can thereby take time for some such children to climb back out again. Given the time, support, encouragement, and patience, they may find more beneficial ways to transcend what they have experienced, and can climb back out.

In essence though, it's harder to undo painful traumatic experiences than to avoid them in the first place, but on the other side of the coin, we mustn't forget that painful experiences can teach us positive ways to respond to situations, especially if our own experiences as children end well through our triumphs.

Yuko and I are heartened by the progress the mothers who experienced so much difficulty have each made with their children since. The challenges they have faced and overcome have inspired these mothers to continue to strive forward as gentle, generous, fully committed supporters of a present and future that best works for their children.

We see their children at our home, amiably playing together with others including our own, socializing and learning new skills and knowledge. I recall one Japanese boy who has taught himself to speak basic English, in combination with his passion for programing classes. While he played, I gave him and our son a kit to build and program a robot arm, which they together spent hours building. Compared to where he'd started, when not wanting to be at school anymore, this to us is a glimpse of his triumph.

Everything happens step-by-step, especially when we provide the facilities and support for onward development, and that includes the important aspect of community for those who homeschool.

I hope this account of the different challenges in our local homeschooling community has been useful. I will now rewind to an earlier beginning of our own story of how Arina chose to start free homeschooling and the more subtle signs which led us to understand it was the right choice for her (and later, for Akira, our son).

Choosing to give school a chance, despite our misgivings, we enrolled Arina at our local primary school as a first year student.

This facility was planned for closure within five years. For us, this was more attractive. Here, her class size meant there would only be seven or eight children for a given year group, per teacher.

The contrast between a Steiner-style kindergarten and a state-run primary school was immediately markedly different. Gone was the focus on learning through fun. Instead, although easy at first, I could observe the teaching was to be primarily focused on repetitive memorization. It was clear the other Japanese parents of children, having been schooled the same way through their own childhoods, saw nothing of concern.

We looked at the food, which was no longer as healthy as it had been at the kindergarten. Now the children ate at their own desks, spread around the classroom, while facing the blackboard (this being even before the Coronavirus era had begun).

I was shocked to find that even during their first year at seven years of age, the children only had 20 minutes of free play time, where they could socialize.

I attended the school sports day a few months after Arina first joined, and recalled the fun of my own primary school sports day activities. When I was a young boy, we'd have wheelbarrow, egg and spoon, beanbag and other games, none of which were included on this day. Instead, the children were forced to jog long distances in sports classes and there were 100m races, relays, etc.

All in the name of toughening them up, I wondered? Gone was the focus on healthy foods prepared each day by the mothers of the kindergarten, instead replaced by poor quality processed non-organic foods, often frozen or from cans, with plenty of processed sugars too.

Mostly, though, I was saddened in seeing how militaristic the style of schooling was for the children. Where was the liberty and fun? Most importantly, would Arina enjoy this schooling? We became increasingly unsure. Having been through it herself, Yuko was more willing to try. I'd already pretty much made my mind up, but the decision wasn't mine to make. Most important was how our daughter felt.

If we made the choice for her to not attend school, someday she might blame us for making the choice she didn't want. I'd already seen this happen with some of the homeschooled children of our older and more experienced homeschooler parent friends.

While at kindergarten, Arina had gained and developed a strong interest in art, but now I could see her creativity was waning—fast. I recalled how polite and well behaved I'd always found Japanese children before having our own, but now I began to see the reasons why. It was because of the conditioning they were subject to throughout school. Not necessarily bad, as being polite, courteous, and considerate of others is a desirable attribute, surely. But what if the costs exceed the benefits and children became very unhappy?

Comparing my own childhood and upbringing, I could see so much that was unnatural. Children shouldn't be made to remain silent and composed when in public, shy and unengaged with what is happening around them. Surely they should be free to express themselves, albeit while encouraging them to communicate politely, rather than boisterously.

In the first year Arina went to the local primary school, she enjoyed it. She was naturally adaptive and a fast learner. Also being someone who finds it important to put sincere effort into the tasks she sets herself to, she was usually top of her class.

Waking up at 6:30 am so she could be at school by 7:30 am, I'd be the one to take her to school in the mornings, while Yuko would sleep a little more, also having to drive 20km and often spend the day with Akira at Asoubimura's Steiner kindergarten.

Despite Arina's visible response as a result to food allergies, she had to get a doctor's note to say that she shouldn't be made to drink milk. She'd not been made to drink it at home, because we could see the effects. Why did we have to prove she was allergic, I wondered?

I remembered her younger years of having loved to sleep and now felt saddened that she'd have to get up so early so she could be at school earlier than the deadline, even at her own insistence (this was, I later learned, part of the militaristic conditioning).

I'd often ask how she felt about school, what she was learning and how her friends were, and at first she'd always say she liked it.

As she started the second year and there was increasingly more memorization, we began to notice the enthusiasm and delight that used to exist disappear from her eyes.

Her drawing activity had slowed, but continued to improve into her second year. Being a fan of Disney, she had liked drawing beautiful mermaids, but now we were seeing fewer and fewer sketches. Her creativity and fun from learning was clearly waning and conformity was becoming the main flavor of how she was being taught to behave. What she mostly looked forward to, she told us, was walking home with her friend who lived nearby, despite carrying a heavy satchel loaded with books strapped to her back.

One day, my wife showed me several alarming sketches Arina had drawn at home, which we both found to be disturbing. They were of a mermaid having her heart cut out. She'd drawn spirits that were taking her own heart and limbs, and she'd also drawn mermaids cut in half.

Over time, I'd been gently letting her know that if she should ever want to leave school, we would be happy to homeschool her. Now, more than before, I began to share with her what I could see I didn't like about her school. Ultimately, though, I let her know we would always respect and leave the final choice up to her. She became increasingly more vocal about not liking this school.

We felt it important to discuss Arina's thoughts and drawings directly with her teacher and also arranged meetings with the headmaster. Although she'd never been a shy child with any of the adults that would visit our home, including people she didn't know, we noticed she didn't feel comfortable enough to speak at all. She would remain silent and courteous until we left the school. Only when she felt it was safe to do so would she speak freely and vent her frustrations. It seemed to both Yuko and me that she was being conditioned from an early age to be fearful of authority.

Yuko and I have always believed in being honest and not holding back in sharing the truth with our children about how we feel about anything that is important. We continued to gently but regularly affirm that we didn't really approve of her primary school, but that the choice was ultimately up to her. When she was ready, we'd homeschool. Similarly, if at any point she decided she'd like to return to school, we promised we would make arrangements for her to attend the best school we could find/afford.

What I recall Arina did express was that she liked her colleagues and her teacher. What she didn't like was the system of teaching and the inflexibility of school rules—a dramatically different environment from Asoubimura's Steiner-based kindergarten. In her words, which reminded us of the disturbing sketches she'd drawn, "School was taking away my soul."

Arina finally chose to leave school at the end of her second year of primary, having made the choice to stay until she'd completed the end of the school year, so that she wouldn't let her teacher down. She was aged eight.

Our son Akira has always been more stubborn and strong-willed by nature and has a lot more stored energy. He also loves to socialize and make others laugh, which unsurprisingly he showed a talent for from a very young age.

Like his sister, at first he enjoyed primary school, after having spent three years at the same kindergarten. He rebelled earlier, however, unable to stand the boredom of learning things in parrot fashion and being made to stay still, after having spent his kindergarten years actively playing and creating things using his hands. Not being allowed to socialize clearly frustrated him.

He began to cry in the mornings and would plead desperately not to go to school. Sensing he was even less suited to militaristic schooling methods and that the delight in his eyes was also quickly fading, he didn't need to be asked twice what his choice was.

I hope sharing these experiences of how we started homeschooling with our own children will give you a clearer understanding of the sort of challenges parents face, and why ultimately it can become the best choice for children to take. Of course, what I have described occurred in a school environment of Japan, but I expect you'll find some similarities. If you don't and you and your child are happy with the status quo, then so be it. Our opinion is not more valid than yours, and we fully respect that free homeschooling may not be every family's best choice.

In our family's case, Yuko and I feel the most important part of education, which can help our children create success in future, is the ability to build excellent relationships. We felt the time was right for each of them to choose—when they consistently and vehemently no longer felt any desire to attend primary school.

Some parents may think that not being in school with other children is detrimental for children's relationships with others, but the truth is, it's actually quite the opposite in our experience. It's much, much better. The genuine friendships our kids have gone on to build with other homeschoolers, non-homeschooler children, all the way through to adults who visit and do things socially, are all much deeper than they'd have created while attending primary school full time. There is also a lot more they've avoided that children at school are nowadays exposed to, which I'll discuss in another chapter.

With Coronavirus causing so many children around the world to have had their education and friendships with classmates severely disrupted, and where so many are finding that online schooling is not a viable substitute, I'd like to start by saying we can only imagine how difficult it must be to have been thrust into such a situation.

The hardship that many families have been going through is a hugely damaging global problem in these times. It has been and continues to be overwhelming, not only for parents and children of all ages, but grandparents, friends, neighbors, and many more besides.

Although I felt from April 2020 the burdens and costs that would come to bear on humanity would vastly outweigh the perceived benefits, I respect people's opinions and choices to be just as valid and important as my own. Mostly, I feel sorrow for children.

There isn't a precise point at which each parent who homeschools decides it's the right time, and there will be many factors including, but not limited to, the effects of the Coronavirus era, which will be unique to each family's circumstances. I'd say the most important time is when we, meaning parents and children, simply cannot see a better realistic alternative and where the current situation becomes untenable.

Most importantly, we must consider the future our children are living into, and thereby equip them with learning that can enhance their lives, so they will be able to create lives they love and are truly inspired by, not a life of unfulfillment and unhappiness, from not being able to live without fear of others and situations they have no control over.

Consider what you, as a parent, and your child(ren) will look back upon in 10 years. Will you look back and wish we had done things starkly differently, instead of just letting state education largely abandon our children during the Coronavirus era?

Would you prefer your children **not** be subject to lockdowns, social distancing, vaccinations, mask wearing and more, or do you feel that the state's resolve and directions are your choice too?

I'm not here to make parents feel like they're wrong. Whatever you choose is a valid choice. My opinion is only as valid as yours. There is no wrong answer; if you do the best with what you know, that's the best you can do, but I would encourage you to never stop asking yourself how you can help your child's life be a better one. It's only natural for a parent to want such.

It's easy for my family to say we picked the right choice in starting homeschooling our own children in their early years, thereby avoiding all the disruption of school closures, endless mask wearing, etc. We look back and see we have made incredible progress, but on the other side of that coin, it took a lot more faith on our part than if we'd been forced, like many parents today, to consider an alternative in the first place.

The alternative of free homeschooling is not a lesser choice to conventional classroom learning. It is, in fact, quite the opposite. The Coronavirus era is a wonderful opportunity to free homeschool, for which there's never been a better time, in our view. Children who are stuck at home can finally learn in much more self-empowering ways.

Once others learn of your progress, some will no doubt be curious and want to know how homeschooled kids are being so empowered and why they're so happy. After all, parents want nothing but the best for their own, and in life, people often follow the example led by others.

As we come to the end of this chapter, I'm sure few of us

will disagree that we are all currently in the midst of severe and unprecedented times for many families and beyond. Some may not yet realize how much their children are missing, or put it out of their minds, as the reality being rolled out may be too challenging for many to face fearlessly.

I acknowledge you, if like us you're a concerned parent who can see the current system is moving toward a permanent state of online schooling. Such schooling style clearly shouldn't become the only and the most effective way to learn for tomorrow's adults, leaders, artisans, businesspeople, teachers, inventors, housewives, entertainers, authors, and more.

We must continue to give children every opportunity to thrive and gain confidence in what they are capable of and inspired by if they're to have bright futures.

Now is the time to make every difference we must for humanity, and certainly not the time to give up. There's a huge amount of wealth to be absorbed in free homeschooling, and from our own experiences and all that we've learned along the way, we have a lot of great knowledge to get through and share with you.

I'm sure you and your children will find the possibilities very liberating and exciting. But to take advantage of infinite possibilities that are waiting to be discovered, first, you and yours have an important choice to consider and make together. What will your family choose?

The best time to start homeschooling has already passed. The next-best time is now.

3 Pros and Cons of Homeschooling

For any concerned parent now, there are many questions that will come to mind when first considering homeschooling, or even free homeschooling. It would be impossible to answer them all, let alone fully. Each of our children and our family circumstances are different, although this in itself contains the answer of what our task in free homeschooling is: We must tailor the learning to best serve our child, not the other way around.

We feel the need to do our utmost to provide the best we can for our children, but hand-in-hand, we must be willing to face the challenges of making mistakes and learning from them.

Of course many parents don't want to risk getting it wrong, but I wonder how many will look deeply and ask themselves if they're considering making a decision to free homeschool out of fear, love for their children, or perhaps even both? I would encourage you to recognize your fears, take a deep breath and let them be. Fear is debilitating and stops us in our tracks, but our greatest achievements are seldom a result of fear.

This book is primarily aimed at pre-high school aged children, which would be the opportune time most parents would seriously consider homeschooling.

For my family, I am amply encouraged to know that for our own children and what we've seen of their progress so far, unless they choose to return to school permanently in future, they are likely to continue homeschooling till senior high school or university (should they choose to continue to further their education as they reach adulthood).

But first things first. Let's address the most common questions parents of would-be homeschoolers ask. I will answer each of them one by one as best I can. In this way, I intend by the end of this chapter to have given a wealth of knowledge and experience, which can help you and your child(ren) find your paths going forward.

WHAT ARE THE BIGGEST FEARS IN FREE HOMESCHOOLING?

Most questions from would-be homeschooling parents come from a premise of caution, or fears based on unknowns, so I will do my best to address and discuss the most common ones.

WILL MY KIDS BECOME SOCIAL OUTCASTS?

For us, the most persistent fear before we started was that our children might go in such different directions from other children, if allowed and encouraged to study subjects they were particularly passionate about. We were afraid they might become weird outcasts by the time they reach adulthood.

There is no indication of this that we have seen, either in our children or in others we know, some of whom are now adults each now into differing walks of life.

With our own, I'd say quite the opposite: Their individual abilities to befriend others and have meaningful conversations that leave lasting impressions continuously encourage our conviction that free homeschooling strengthens a child's abilities to create relationships. They each have excellent engaging abilities to befriend people of all ages and spark lasting relationships.

Adults often comment on how eloquently and thoughtfully our children communicate and converse about a wide variety of subjects they are interested in. Most homeschooled children we know have excellent social skills, which are a vital ingredient for progress throughout life, both socially and professionally. Fact is, provided we parents are willing to take them to meet and be with others, or invite them into our homes, the opportunities for socializing will be more than ample.

WILL OTHERS THINK BADLY OF OUR FAMILY FOR HOMESCHOOLING?

We had many people along the way tell us we were making a grave mistake when first considering homeschooling. None of those who advised us against it had any experience of homeschooling, and some of them were even professional teachers.

Neither Yuko nor I let our lives be led by what others think of us. To us, that wouldn't be living our lives by what we're most inspired, but by how others would direct us. This resolve is self-empowering and is simply one's choice, which I must ultimately leave to you to make, but I'll say this: Look carefully at the costs and benefits of your choices.

Being the one taking a lead on facilitating continued learning for our daughter, Yuko strongly believed: "Whether others approve or not isn't of great importance. Your child's most effective and self-beneficial ways of learning should be your main priority."

What I can share is that today, some five years after we first started homeschooling, the progress of our children and others we know doesn't invoke pity from others, but quite the opposite. People, including retired schoolteachers, private music teachers, government ministers and adults from all walks of life whose lives our children's touch, often comment on how amazed they are at their continual progress.

Our daughter won a prestigious national speech contest for up to 21-year-olds in her second language (English) at 10 years of age and left the audience in amazement of her knowledge and calm self-confidence. Interestingly, when she performed her speech, Arina's primary school headmaster traveled for over 90 minutes to attend. Would he have come had be truly believed homeschooling didn't offer a genuine alternative to Japanese primary school?

In recent months, our children have become good friends with a young trainee teacher who has become very interested in starting his own free school once he graduates from university in a year's time. He's seen a possibility through who our kids are.

Provided you and yours are committed and follow what are clearly their passions, you'll stand to make excellent progress in a great many ways that children who go to school are less likely to absorb. Today, the only people who think badly of our kids and homeschooling are the ones who don't yet know them. Naturally, we're not ashamed to share the truth.

HOW EARLY CAN YOU START HOMESCHOOLING?

Homeschooling can start as early as parents want and, indeed, can work alongside conventional schooling. It can, naturally, also start as late as might work for your family and for as long or as short a time that is beneficial. We know parents with several children who have never attended state or private schools, and parents whose children started quite late. It's really what works best for your family.

IS IT EASY TO HOMESCHOOL YOUR CHILDREN?

This is a question that is difficult if not impossible to quantify, and as we've learned from experience, it depends largely on the parents and how they direct themselves. It also depends on each individual child. Girls can be easier to direct and seem to be willing to learn earlier, whereas boys tend to want to spend more time playing, especially when they're younger (don't underestimate the learning power of play. Children learn a lot while playing!)

But then boys pick up later, as they can often become more focused on particular subjects than girls, but of course I am generalizing here.

My own greatest challenge in homeschooling our kids has been learning to be patient and in acknowledging our children more. They thrive on having their achievements recognized! I also sometimes find myself anticipating that they should learn all that I had to by the time I was their age. Being softer, like their mother, has been my biggest challenge, which I continue to face regularly.

It's better to facilitate materials and facilities which keep their passions lit than to try to impose what they must do as far as possible. I'll elaborate more on this later.

Homeschooling requires a lot more commitment than simply kissing the kids goodbye each morning and letting someone else take on all the responsibility (or not, in the case of schools being closed and schooling moving to online tuition, which seems rife with problems for many, we're told. We have no experience of this, since schools in Japan have remained open through much of the Coronavirus period). Free homeschooling requires a lot more time invested in our children and spent together with them and I would best describe it as a parent's labor of love. Once again, provided you and yours are committed and follow what are clearly their passions, you'll make excellent progress in a great many ways that a child who goes to school is less likely to absorb.

HOW DO HOMESCHOOLED CHILDREN MAKE FRIENDS?

I know we had this concern at first. Our daughter lost her best friend at school when she chose to leave and was sad at first, and eventually lost contact with her other classmates too. But her older friends from Asoubimura endured.

We didn't just stop there. Soon after Arina first began homeschooling, Yuko spent time searching locally for activities she could do where she'd befriend others. She joined a swimming course and continued her ballet. She took on piano and singing courses (music being something she continues to be particularly passionate about).

One of our friends recommended meeting Akio Furuyama when we first began seriously considering homeschooling for Arina. He was known to have successfully tutored other homeschoolers for decades and is very well known in homeschooling circles of Japan. Furuyama San knew many other homeschoolers and already had a community around him.

Upon visiting our home, surrounded by old forest and a lot of open space, combined with parents who were eager to welcome other children to share our facilities, he began to create events where children regularly came to our home to play. In addition, Arina (then later Akira) would go to study and play in other homeschoolers' homes.

As her interests deepened into music and developed, she continued to take her own directions, rather than follow others, and began being invited to sing at jazz venues. As mentioned, she won the Kokorozashi speech contest, and from that she made friends not just at the event, but met many others who'd heard of her success, and later asked her to present and speak at other events (online and in person), live. She likes to make jewelry and makes friends through this hobby too. Everywhere she goes, she makes new friends.

Akira is clearly not interested in the same things as his sister, but has of course made friends with the homeschooling kids we had already befriended. He's also had more success in keeping in touch with his school friends. We've taken his best old school friend with us camping during summer holidays and sometimes he comes over to play after school (and has mentioned he likes playing with Akira most, as all his other friends are addicted to computer games and don't have much interest in playing normally anymore).

Akira's hobbies at nine years of age are in making things (he's a natural engineer, much like his father) and tinkering with mechanical and electrical components. Some days, after his basic studies, he'll be making a hovercraft, other days learning to skateboard. Another day I'll find him using a magnifying glass in the sunlight to try to start a small (supervised) fire. On another day he'll be making a new model airplane that he's designed. It's through play like this that boys can develop their knowledge and confidence in their abilities.

For his birthday, knowing he and I share an interest in sports cars, speed and mechanical things, I bought him an old junior racing go-cart, which together we restored over the course of two evenings. At first, I'd thought to work on it alone and present it as a ready-to-use gift, but asked him. He far preferred to tinker with it and learn. And so, we did—together.

The first time he used it, it still didn't run properly, so together we fixed it. In the space of three weeks, he'd made five new friends, one of whose fathers gave us two more (adult) carts, so that I could also go carting with Akira. In the space of just six months, he's learned a huge amount, and declares he is intent on becoming a professional racing driver. Indeed, his progress as a driver is remarkable, and even on the local track he's made friends of all ages.

Hobbies shared are not to be underestimated, despite their costs, as ways to cement strong bonds between parent and child. Hobbies are a great way to meet like-minded friends too. Along the way, he's learned valuable knowledge of engineering, physics, and even English vocabulary, while developing his new passion for racing carts.

Despite Coronavirus, our kids get out a lot and see plenty of other children. Their conversational abilities and passions for the things they're interested in naturally build friendships with people they meet, young or old. At no point have our children said they regret leaving school because they can't make friends.

Truth is, they play a lot more with others than they would if they were in Japanese schools, and given the same approach, combined with the considerable growth in homeschooling during this Coronavirus era, I'm sure homeschooling children can find a lot more other children to befriend if their parents are mindful of the important benefits of fun socialization for children.

IS IT POSSIBLE TO HOMESCHOOL WHILE WORKING FULL TIME?

I've mulled this question on a personal level. Yes, I do work full time, but have been self-employed for 22 years and we are fortunate that Yuko can dedicate her time to being a dedicated housewife.

What about single parents, or two-parent working families? Nobody could possibly deny such scenarios present some serious challenges, but are such situations untenable for homeschooling?

First, I think it's important to look at the costs and benefits of homeschooling before answering that question. How committed are you to ensuring your child has the best education he can possibly get? I don't necessarily mean in a purely academic sense, but a social sense too, where a healthy and strongly supportive family structure is an important aspect of childhood experience that will give a great return in building a successful future for your son or daughter.

Clearly, most of us need money to live, and we're in a time where earning money threatens to become even more difficult. It's easy to fall into the whirlpool of fear and desperation in such times and believe we're not capable of more.

One of the first and foremost steps (see sub-chapter Seven Steps to Free Homeschool Success) we encourage new homeschoolers to make is to establish themselves within the local homeschool community. There are quite possibly other local single-parent homeschoolers you'll meet who may have found trusted people within your community with whom they share the responsibilities of caring for children while single parents work full, or part time.

If you're committed, there's a strong likelihood you will find a way, so we would encourage you to explore fully to find out what's possible. We've witnessed wonderful homeschooling success stories by single mothers here in Japan, despite Japan not having a great social security system and single mothers thereby having to make do with very little income.

What makes the challenges for some of them easier to overcome is the natural community support that exists in the countryside. People will rent old unused homes cheaply, local farmers will befriend and share some of their produce for free, while some will employ the mothers part time, and even allow their children to be present when they're still too young to stay at home independently. Mothers train part time and become self-employed.

There are always ways in which we can reinvent ourselves in the face of challenges. The only ones really stopping us from making breakthroughs are ourselves and the beliefs we live into.

During the pandemic of 2020, my income was severely hit, with sizable business investments I had made for anticipated tourism in Japan's 2020 Olympics at an almost complete standstill. Still, homeschooling certainly works for our children, and I am continuing to work where I can to make an income to support them and Yuko.

We grow our own vegetables and fruits organically, while keeping some livestock (another great aspect of learning to be self-sustainable, which may be useful for your children's future).

Learn what is your truth. Be wise, be unstoppable. Be your children's hero. In the face of a challenge, or even in times of failure, I would strongly urge you to investigate all that is possible for you and your family and always be making progress.

HOW MUCH DOES HOMESCHOOLING COST?

There is great flexibility in costs of homeschooling, especially for families who don't have much, if any, spare money. Finding ingenious ways to participate in beneficial studying of what the children are interested in offers great learning experiences—possibly better than for families with ample financial resources to draw from.

If you're already challenged to meet your financial needs, and your children are not being fed in school each day, costs of food are bound to rise. On the other side of the coin, you may have space in a garden, or a community space where food can be grown, or find a plot whose owner you befriend.

You and the children could volunteer as part-time woofers at a nearby permaculture project, etc. There is a lot of wealth to be learned in knowing about growing natural foods and developing a hands-on relationship with nature. This instills a natural wisdom in children too. Nature is overflowing in gentle ways of teaching wise old ways.

Libraries offer lots of learning opportunities too. Many books are available online. By tapping into local like-minded communities, or creating them (online, hopefully evolving into face-to-face) if they don't already exist, families can share of their resources and what they discover.

Hobbies can often help develop great talent and learnings, which might otherwise never be realized. Buying our daughter a DIY jewelry kit at five years of age led to her development of amazing skills in design, where she buys her own raw materials online for small change, makes beautiful pieces, then sells them at fairs and online at a profit, while gradually learning to become financially independent.

With our son, I intend to show him how to make small parts to modify and improve cars and sell them online to make a profit. If he's interested, together we'll learn how 3D plastic printing is done, and thereby make parts for projects to sell, etc.

These things cost a little money but can be very beneficial for learning. Always look at costs and benefits and encourage children to be interested in learning how to earn their pocket money, then develop ways to invest it well.

Such things as above can be fun on an individual level, but may encourage and facilitate further development. Never forget that in community is resilience, so build it around yourself (and please do join ours which we are in the process of building).

We share a growing list of great books and learning resources as part of our final chapter, on our website www.howtohomeschool.life

Find people in your local community who you can help. Old people may need food cooked for them. Involve the children, and in turn the elderly may offer to share some of their life experiences, and perhaps even share their hobbies and passions and instill them in your children. They may be happy to pay for the benefits of having others care for and spend time with them too—much nicer than being in a home, gazing alone out of a window, or being forced to do what they don't want to, wouldn't you say?

Children are delightful when around elderly people. Such community is natural, provided all participants are able and willing to share and enjoy the mutual benefits.

For parents with sparse financial means, other possibilities for the children may also be possible and can be surprisingly inexpensive. We've enrolled our children in such communal activities as singing lessons, swimming, dance, ballet, skate parks, etc. Where some parents don't have the financial means to pay for small things, we encourage our children to share their hobbies, materials, and facilities with others. A lot of costs can be offset by helping others. Plant seeds of possibility, everywhere!

IS HOMESCHOOL A LEGITIMATE EDUCATION?

A legitimate education is, one could presume, what some would refer to as a typical state school education. To answer this question, we might first consider why school education was created, and where the world is currently headed, to consider its current relevance.

School education only started around 200 years ago, and became widespread to facilitate the creation of a workforce for the First Industrial Revolution, which was sparked by the invention of the steam engine in the late 1700s.

The Second Industrial Revolution occurred roughly 100 years later, in the late 1800s, with mass production becoming widespread, and that was where school education became a "norm," where electricity and fossil fuels fueled further rapid growth, and with it, the start of consumerism.

The Third Industrial Revolution began in the 1980s, with the widespread adoption of computers, followed by the internet, and along with it, a huge move toward personal debt and uncontrolled consumerism, which could never be infinitely sustainable. Something had to give, at some point.

For some of us who see it, we are now at the forefront of the Fourth Industrial Revolution, where information and artificial intelligence is already leading to the disappearance of a large number of, until recently, viable jobs.

Yuko and I began asking ourselves why our local education system here in Japan (and similarly in other First World countries elsewhere) was educating children to be good at following instructions, to work for others. Who will they work for in future?

57

Jobs such as manufacturing, face-to-face retail sales, driving, and many others besides seem to be in decline, especially as IT is already able to replace workers.

Ignoring the many issues that would be likely to develop, the so called "Great Reset" is being rolled out as the answer to our future problems, while it takes younger generations, seemingly without choice, toward a future of having far fewer jobs.

During these Coronavirus times, children may have the choice to study online. I believe as cost-cutting measures continually bite, and teachers feel more comfortable working from home, online schooling may increasingly become the norm for the majority.

For some parents this may be the right answer. For others, such as Yuko and me, online schooling as a one-size-fits-hundreds would not be the most beneficial choice to make for our kids.

We see what we are facing during these challenging times as a call to provide our children with evolved ways of learning, where at an early stage of their lives they may learn excellence in the development of knowledge and skills that most strongly resonate within them. When we are excellent at doing something that others are unable to do, or lack the talent for, an opportunity for their career may present itself.

I see a clear advantage for homeschoolers who start earliest in naturally absorbing skills, gaining knowledge on how to live life effectively and happily, and doing what they love, compared to kids who are often generally disinterested in school, and instead of developing good social skills, spend their spare time on social media, or playing games. This in itself is a pandemic.

I believe individuals who develop early interests and passions are much more likely to go on to live happy, fulfilled and professional lives than people who unwillingly study subjects they have little interest in. People who are good at passing exams may be construed as successful. Many of us will know such people, but in my own experience, I don't know many who are truly happy in their careers. Do you?

Times are changing fast. Many of us are coming to realize the current state education in most countries isn't nearly keeping up with the requirements for the future. We believe homeschooling offers the best currently possible option for most people, who realize that the best way forward is for each of us to make as big a difference in this world as we can, and to share the benefits of such as the adults of tomorrow.

HOW DO HOMESCHOOLED KIDS END UP IN LIFE?

This is an often asked question, which might be better phrased and answered in the context of, "How will homeschooled kids fare in life, after the intended 'Great Reset' that government leaders continuously mention?"

If you haven't yet seen what is being rolled out, i.e. the Fourth Industrial Revolution and the Great Reset, you may even disagree with me. Please understand I'm not here to belittle the choices of others. Nobody knows for sure exactly how things are going to play out, and personally speaking, I prefer to accept all differing opinions to be just as valid as my own.

We're all doing the best we can with what we know, and the vast majority want the same. To be able to make good life choices, is it better to empower children through learning to make important choices from as young as possible, or is it better to shelter them from such until they are adults and out in the world on their own? Which will give them better skills at choosing what to do in life?

Is it better to let them learn as much as possible, from a perspective of sincere interest, passion, discussion and being part of a community with like-minded individuals, or to put them into (possibly online, for a currently indeterminable period going forward) one-size-fits-all styled learning?

In free homeschooling, children develop at speed while playing outside, particularly when surrounded by nature, and where they learn through what (and who) most inspires them. This is what free homeschooling can offer in abundance.

As we've seen early on with our own and other kids, natural learning builds self-confidence and gumption that will serve them well throughout adulthood. Here, learning, study, and development is a part of day-to-day life, which is likely to continue far beyond childhood. Your child can learn his or her true identity and see the people and activities they most resonate with.

Comparing to the widely accepted alternative, where conventional classroom learning of curricular subjects can be driven in some children through regular tests, in the less inspired children, tests can instill fear of failure and a belief in one's own ineptitude (where they may simply not have been ready to learn that particular subject yet).

Most schoolchildren learn to be afraid of failure, rather than deeply understanding that failure is an intrinsic and core part of effective learning and development. Is failure therefore not to be welcomed? Which will help in the development of an effective, fulfilled adult's life? Knowing one's own identity well and at what we are most gifted and happiest doing, or working hard (or not) to avoid failure?

There are many successful homeschooled adults, some of whom made history and are internationally famous today: Thomas Edison, Isaac Newton, Theodore Roosevelt, Agatha Christie, Hans Christian Anderson, Soichiro Honda, and on a more recent note, as names children will recognize: Selena Gomez and Justin Timberlake, to name just a handful. There are many, many more.

DO YOU REGRET HOMESCHOOLING KIDS?

Honestly, the only time I've seen any evidence of this is when a friend's elder son questioned his parent's homeschooling choices, as an adult, remembering that he wasn't ever given the choice to go to conventional state school.

Provided we make sure it is our child's choice not to attend school, but to instead stay at home (choice of the child to not attend school being a legal requirement in Japan) is not only empowering for the child, but should also avoid such scenarios as the one described above.

Of all the other free homeschooled children we've met thus far, all prefer learning at home and their parents share that sentiment. Of the adults we know who have been homeschooled, I also see no regrets, aside from those which many of us adults carry, of wishing they'd spent more time learning, and not avoiding it.

In our eyes, when a child isn't interested in learning something, it's either the wrong time, and usually better to be patient, or it demonstrates that the ways in which they're learning may not be most beneficial to them. In such cases, it is better to find a more interesting approach.

WHAT IS A TYPICAL FREE HOMESCHOOL CURRICULUM?

The simplest answer I could give would be, "There isn't one," but this would leave the reader cold, without an explanation.

Let's first look at what free homeschooling is not: It is not a one-size-fits-all curriculum that is taught by one teacher, in a classroom. It's not a direct equivalent to attending school.

Free homeschooling is an alternative, where a curriculum is individually tailored whilst being flexible to meet the learning needs each child is most inspired by.

Although not necessarily what will work for each family, our kids follow the workbooks used in Japanese primary school for their given school year. Local schoolteachers pass these on to us, for Japanese Kanji and mathematics mainly. These are just the core basics of which they can complete a year's supply by working through a couple of exercises each morning.

We give examples in things they see in day-to-day life, so they understand the needs and benefits of learning to the core basics. For example, our son knows he's good at engineering. To share his ideas with others, clearly he'll need to explain dimensions, and write well, so he continues to learn at his pace. Sometimes, it's slow, sometimes he learns remarkably fast.

The rest of our children's learnings are centered around their interests. Our daughter likes reading romantic novels and Japanese Manga books. Our son is currently interested in powered flight and designing airplanes, then flying them (including inexpensive remote-controlled gliders), as well as reading about go-cart racing and driving techniques. They read English books on subjects that interest them most, some of which were written for adults. We actively encourage them to read. They're both fluently bilingual, without ever having had formal tuition, and Japanese who notice the ease with which they speak, read and write English are often amazed.

They're both good at and enjoy mathematical challenges, and recently discovered the Rubik's Cube. I've also taught Akira to play chess, which he now enjoys and asks me to play, instead of watching a movie. It's a great way to enjoy learning how to strategize and using one's imagination to figure out how to beat your opponent. Backgammon is another great game, useful for learning basic arithmetic while having a lot of fun. There are infinite ways to learn while enjoying our time together.

Other times, they might read a recipe book and make a delicious dessert. Most play and discovery as children offers a form of learning, and you'll be amazed at how one thing leads to another as they continue to explore.

IF HOMESCHOOLED CHILDREN DECIDE TO RETURN TO SCHOOL, DO THEY INTEGRATE WELL?

This is another question we've asked ourselves.

Arina decided in 2019 she'd like to live abroad and learn a third language with which to continue her development of knowledge. Our ethos is that we will do our best to facilitate whatever our children are truly inspired to do, provided it isn't dangerous. Pre-pandemic, I had committed myself to making this financially possible.

Alas, Coronavirus put a stop to ideas of her living and studying abroad. In the end, she decided to spend a year living with a host family on Tokashiki, a sub-tropical island in Okinawa, population 700, which she loves. I've asked her recently if she'll continue there next year. I was surprised to hear that, although she loves her life in Tokashiki, she will probably choose to return to free schooling here at home, where she can follow her deepest interests and passions.

I digress. In answer to this question, I'd say a resounding "Yes!" regarding our children, given how well they strike up relationships with other children and adults of all ages. Clearly this also depends on the child and how they learn about relationships, while learning and developing in a free homeschooling environment.

Most homeschooled children we know are generally more confident and a lot less shy than children of the same ages who attend local school. Our children also tend to have a broader scope of knowledge and abilities, which other children and adults find intriguing.

The next chapter delves deeper and shares more of our children's story of inspired free homeschool learning.

4 What is Free Homeschooling?

At first, we didn't really know how
we'd homeschool. We just believed in
our hearts this was the right choice,
and being fully committed, we would
find the best solutions.

Here I'll share some of our experiences from which we hope you will understand and begin to see possibilities of how you can create similar homeschooling for your own growing family, from the context of "freedom to be."

We have two very different children, aged three years apart. Arina is now 12, and Akira is aged nine.

Arina is naturally careful to avoid problems and dangers. A willing listener, she is a strong-willed character with strong ability to concentrate her mind. She values time to herself and has always shown herself to be a thinker. She gravitates more toward the arts.

Arina is good at making relationships with others, and like many girls, tends to prefer to concentrate on quality of individual friendships than being the life of the party. She had been a top student in her first couple of years at primary school, and latterly, after five years of free homeschooling, is top of her class during her current stint homestaying on Tokashiki island and attending school there. Everything she really puts her mind to she seems to excel at. Arina is naturally quite tidy and organized.

Akira is quite the polar opposite. He is excitable and enthusiastic about whatever he's interested in, in the moment, but is easily distracted. When younger, he'd forget what he'd be doing one moment, and quickly get so engrossed in the next that he would forget to tidy things away, leaving a trail of toys, materials, and other things in his wake.

At primary school, he'd have a short attention span, but we observed where he's very interested in something, he can dedicate an entire day and night working on a project. Some might call this ADHD (which wasn't even a term when I was a child). We feel it's just his natural way. He's young, energetic, and is driven by enthusiasm.

Sensing our concerns, we were told by our homeschooling mentor, Furuyama San, that Akira would calm down as he got older.

This year we're observing our son's continued development into his second year of homeschooling. Now, provided it interests him, he will be still and read a book for long periods. He's becoming tidier too, understanding this to be an important factor if he wants to be successful in building projects successfully, and he's finally gained an interest in mathematics now he realizes he can use what he's learning.

He's more self-disciplined and is learning Chinese characters, to complement his Japanese comprehension abilities.

He's stubborn and not always a great listener. He can persevere endlessly until he finds the answer to the challenge he has set himself. He learns best from "doing" things, and from what he observes. Akira gravitates more toward the sciences and has a natural interest and early aptitude for engineering. He's good at making friendships and has charm and a natural ability in creating them. Akira was opposite to his sister. Untidy and disorganized, but he's changing— thankfully.

How have we made progress with our two? Yes, indeed!

Arina began homeschooling a year before her younger brother Akira finished his final year of kindergarten. We'd been forewarned by Furuyama San that when leaving school, most children need time to adjust and reacquaint themselves with real freedom to learn. On average, he said, we could expect it may take one month to unschool per year studied.

Depending on how far and hard they feel they've been pushed in directions against their nature, children naturally need the grace of time to settle into their new roles. It's the opportune time to give them space and time to play and redevelop or begin to discover their greatest passions.

In hindsight, being introduced to Yukio Furuyama, with over three decades of experience and a passion for natural learning, was a very important first step for us. Furuyama San is currently writing another book, which is to be published in Japanese. I do hope we can persuade him to have it translated. He has a great amount of knowledge that can help us all.

I would similarly strongly recommend building a great community of knowledgeable and experienced people around you who understand the difficulties and challenges some children face in attending school, and are committed to making a profound difference—as early as possible.

Furuyama San was able to advise and help us avoid the pitfalls that beginner homeschoolers make, but also gave us valuable advice.

Meeting him was manifested through Yuko's diligence in searching and speaking with others, to work out what would be the best way forward. When hearing of our commitment and sincere stand for better schooling, someone offered to make the introduction.

We realize not all parents may have the facilities we're blessed with. We warmly encourage you to sign up for the free chapter at the end of this book, so we can invite you and your children to join us for future intended podcasts, video courses and webinars, as we build our intended community.

Naturally, one of our first thoughts was about our daughter's development of social skills.

Furuyama San, being a tutor familiar with many homeschoolers, visited us just as we were taking a leap of faith. We still didn't know.

Upon seeing our home surrounded by large forested land, he suggested it would be a perfect venue to host children regularly. He could see the possibility that aligned with ours.

When we bought this old home, we knew then that God had made it possible, not just for us, but the future we'd create, even though I didn't know just how it would go—such is the power of free choice. Creating a localized homeschool community space was one way in which socialization for children, including our own, would continue to develop.

We all learn through making mistakes, and this includes our conduct as parents. Mistakes are something we all must welcome, a necessary and natural occurrence along the path of progress.

As our son Akira has learned, and I sometimes ask him to recall, **"A mistake is only a mistake when I refuse to correct it."**

It is important to be conscious not just of the continuously developing interests of our children, but how our own past can influence our own thought processes, whether constructively, or detrimentally, toward them.

We can be very affected by the fear of them not being good enough or failing, with the possibility of employing the same tactics to coerce our children to learn as we likely experienced in our own childhoods.

At first, Yuko felt it important that Arina didn't fall behind on memorizing and learning the calligraphy of Chinese Kanji characters, or her mathematics. We felt she needed to keep up with the school curriculum! They would spend a lot of time together, Yuko coaching Arina daily to keep up to date with her drill books.

There were many tears and frustrating mornings for both mother and daughter, as Arina would find this a very uninspiring way to learn. Yuko watched, listened, and continued to think, while communicating with others of a lot more experience.

We realized, partly through Furuyama San's coaching, that our train of thought on how to teach stemmed from our own insecurities, rather than our daughter's actual needs.

Yuko thereafter eased up; Arina really didn't need to keep up with the exact pace of school. We instead began to feel it would be desirable, if not essential, to learn to write and read eloquently. For a homeschooler, this should be at a pace that works on a personal level, while continuously striving to keep it as fun and interesting as possible.

So we began to realize that homeschooling is clearly not a rigid scenario of "one-size-fits-all." Instead, it is the wonderful opportunity to create a bespoke learning environment that suits each child, to access and maximize the learning that is waiting to be discovered individually, when the time is right.

We have also observed and learned that often the timing isn't right—and what doesn't interest a child when we deem it to be the right time is because it's not inspiring, and there may be something she'd benefit more from naturally learning at this time, or we may need to make it more interesting.

Arina has a strong natural interest in drawing and art, so one of the first lessons together with Yuko, without the constraints of a school curriculum, was to study the Statue of Liberty in NYC. They learned of the historic relationship between France and America toward the end of the 1800s and the significance of the statue. Arina explored how it was built, delivered, and erected in its location.

These were things that fascinated Arina. With relatively little effort, here she was learning bits of history and geography while simultaneously developing her reading of Japanese and writing about what she and Yuko learned together. The tears and upsets stopped and now, instead, she lost track of time and was clearly enjoying the experiences of learning at home.

She continued her drills at a slower pace. I pointed out that more and more, calligraphy, or Japanese handwriting, were unlikely to be important in future, as computers and hand-held devices might make writing by hand largely obsolete by the time our children reach adulthood.

Learning mathematics (development of logic skills) and Japanese reading were a practical necessity and she understood and accepted these would be essential, but nonetheless, we continued to concentrate on making learning more fun than she'd experienced at school, all the while monitoring her interest and happiness.

Yuko would regularly take Arina to the library, where she'd choose 20 books at a time, in any subject she found to be of interest in the children's section. Naturally, she soon ran out of books to read.

Prior to the beginning of her homeschooling, I too had started to consider how best I could teach our children. Firstly, with English as my primary spoken language, I wanted to pass this on. From as soon as each of our children had begun to speak, I've nearly always spoken with them in English, being unafraid to use "big" words.

Through the gentle urging of my closest friends, and this book's editor's wife who was an international primary school teacher in Tokyo at the time, we'd learned about "Phonics" books as a great method to teach basic reading skills. Working through them, while capitalizing on an interest instilled through bedtime stories, by the time she was six, Arina could read simple children's books by herself, in English as a second language.

At eight years old, she began reading novels for children of her age, these also now being a part of her homeschooling curriculum. Being her second language, she began with a couple of pages a day, then gradually more and more as she became increasingly familiar with previously unknown words. She naturally figured out the meanings of the few words she didn't understand, and found herself growing to also enjoy reading in English.

Next was writing, which she continues to learn, but already she's had such a head start in a foreign language that her own English skills were on par and have now excelled those of her school's full-time English teacher.

We began to introduce Arina to every activity we could afford that she thoroughly enjoyed, from dancing and ballet, through playing musical instruments, and then swimming lessons. These activities also gave her access to other children of the same age, where she'd make friends.

And so the learning continued in the directions that suited her most, and through seeing great progress, our fears of failure and the unknowns gradually fell by the wayside. Friends and family saw how well she was growing up and would comment positively too.

Whilst Yuko felt the need to coach her daily over that first year, Arina increasingly developed as an independent learner. Through knowing the things she wanted and needed to do, she also began to understand that she could be self-motivated, rather than awaiting instruction each day. This was her own, rather than a conventional school environment.

Yuko still needed to be by her side from time to time and both of us made ourselves available to help and discuss, if required, to ensure she has support whenever she needed it in understanding what she's looking at. For example, with mathematics exercises.

That first year of homeschooling for Arina rolled by, and Akira finished his kindergarten of the natural kind of learning that had so benefited his sister.

We'd noticed many differences in their interests during Akira's three years at Asoubimura. Where Arina had been excellent at singing, dancing and participating in Asoubimura's theatrical events, with total focus and a natural aptitude to sing in tune, Akira would be easily distracted and was not at all coordinated with others. He did make us all laugh, at just how disinterested he was! We'd noticed he was a lot more interested in making toys, using small pieces of wood and nails, or getting up to mischief.

He'd developed the great ability to make others laugh, and had always loved to converse and interact with others, and so it was natural he became very good at befriending and playing with other children.

He was always super-energetic and would charge from place to place at full speed. This led to his learning to ride a bicycle not long after he'd learned to speak, aged just two. I observed speed and propulsion was something he clearly enjoyed, and just like his papa, he had developed a love for cars by the time he could speak.

By the time he was finished with Asoubimura, aged six, he had developed a lot.

At graduation, we weren't as enthusiastic about the idea of homeschooling him. We felt, now having some experience under our belts, that he was likely to be more difficult to homeschool, not least because there wouldn't be just one child, but now two to homeschool simultaneously.

Just as with Arina, Akira went to the same local primary school. Even though Arina had chosen to homeschool, this didn't mean her brother would choose the same, and we reasoned if he ever did, it would also have to be his choice. We discussed that whilst the door would always be open for him to choose, it might benefit him to get some discipline at school, and to be taught the basics of reading Japanese.

Unlike Arina, he showed no early interest in reading English, and although I tried, I didn't force him. Doing so could be counterproductive, and might make English reading unattractive for the future. Instead, I continued to try and inspire him to learn, through reading picture books at bedtime, which I believed he'd enjoy.

Enrolling in his new school, he was excited at the prospect of joining a new place of learning and making new friends. Just as he'd seemed eager to leave his mother's belly on the day of his birth, unlike his sister, in the beginning of his first year, he'd be the first in our household to wake up. By 6:30 am he'd often be raring to go to school, even though there was an hour before he should be there.

Being full of energy, but having come from the kindergarten where he'd been able to play in sand for hours each day, splashing in sandy puddles and building things from sand, wood, wool, paper, etc., he was excited and especially enjoyed the walk to school with his friends.

Now, suddenly though, it was his turn to sit in a classroom at a small desk of his own, with seven other children and only 20 minutes of playtime a day and to attend/participate in regimented school assemblies, stiff and inflexible in nature. He was required to look at the blackboard and learn what was being presented, whether he liked it or not. Little wonder that he had a short attention span and would often be found daydreaming, gazing through the window.

The class in which he performed best was English, having learned it naturally at home. Notably, just as we'd noticed with Arina, he at first also felt the need to pretend he was learning something new as a means of conforming to what was expected of him. We were not surprised to find he also excelled at athletics.

Akira continued to attend school daily, but his enthusiasm was clearly waning by the beginning of his second year. Now he began to say he too wanted to homeschool, although we felt it was because he wanted to avoid studying at all, rather than a result of any perceived trauma. He continued attending until he was nearing the end of his third year of primary school when the Covid-19 period meant his school was closed.

With the shut-down periods and ongoing uncertainties resulting, we began his homeschooling while he was unable to attend.

By this time, into her third year of homeschooling, Arina was effectively studying by herself, only wanting our attention when she was stuck with something (we've never stopped monitoring what she's doing, but we also give her the freedom to be self-motivated, provided she's committed and making progress).

Looking back, she had made incredible free homeschooling progress.

Her drawing had matured to a level that professional adult artists and animators were impressed with (the picture on the cover of this book was also drawn by her).

She had entered the Kokorozashi speech presentation conference, just before turning 10 years old. Against 550 other entrants, Arina was selected as one of 12 finalists in 2018, with a moving speech about the environment, presented in Japanese, complete with a PowerPoint presentation containing her pictures.

Undeterred at not winning, she presented in 2019, just before she turned 11, and won. She's the youngest winner ever, where all other finalists have been in their late teens or early 20s.

Kokorozashi was a very strengthening learning experience for her, which is why I mention it again: enroll your children in public speaking competitions, if they're interested. Such events in life can make a profound difference for young children.

When Arina was 10, while we were in Portugal in 2018 to visit family during our summer holiday, Arina and Yuko booked some inexpensive charter flights to Egypt for a week. Arina had a strong interest in ancient Egyptian history and so they spent an intense week touring and studying the amazing sights with the help of a knowledgeable and experienced Egyptian guide who'd arranged a busy schedule. After returning to Portugal, Arina drew pictures of her experiences and wrote an account of her learning there.

Second languages learned at an early age help children to create additional links for brain development, and thereby open a possibility to learn more languages. Wanting both children to learn Portuguese, we enrolled them in a summer camp the following year, and I continue to speak with them in Portuguese from time to time. After all, it's a part of their heritage.

I haven't yet switched from speaking with them primarily in English when we're all together (mostly we converse during family meals), partly because English is a language Yuko is also fluent in, but because we feel it's important to continue to expand Akira's vocabulary, reading, and writing abilities first.

Next year I will change, since Portuguese will make the learning of French, Spanish, and Italian a lot easier, and perhaps the following year, I'll finally stop using English with them at home. Since they both enjoy speaking, it would be another avenue of learning they'd clearly each benefit from. Not least, they both love Portugal, which is also of course a part of their heritage.

Here in Chiba, during the early stages of the declared pandemic, voluntary lockdown only lasted a month, from March to April 2020.

When schools reopened, Akira was most excited to see his friends again at first, but soon grew tired of wearing a mask for most of the day, being socially distanced, wearing face shields and being coerced into doing even more seemingly mindless memorization, to catch up with the missed classes as part of the year's curriculum. Within two weeks, he'd begun to say ever more strongly and desperately that he was now committed to homeschooling, which developed into crying and severe upsets each morning. He was desperate.

Just as for his sister, when we arranged meetings to speak with the staff and headmaster about his wishes, he too found it difficult to speak openly in front of his teacher about why he didn't want to attend school anymore. Being so good at communicating, and someone usually so ready to voice what he didn't want to do, we found it interesting that he too would stay silent in the face of authority. What was this conditioning at school?

With challenges come choices and opportunities, and here was one that we already had the conviction would be the best for our son. We wanted it to absolutely be his choice.

It did take a couple of months for Akira to settle into homeschooling, and even then, he'd try to do the minimum of his reading and math exercises and finish them in record time.

We've observed other free homeschooling parents allow their children to do whatever they please, and most certainly, we know for sure, children do learn naturally. I see it as a weakness in ourselves as parents (especially myself, if I'm entirely honest) that we don't entirely give faith in our children's natural ability to learn what they need by themselves.

I realize this stems from my fear our children might fail in life. During my own childhood, I remember knowing people who worked for my father who'd never learned to read, but who got on fine in life and went on to run small, simple, but successful businesses. I've also seen how a fear of failure can hold people back from being able to learn. These justifications, though, are just that. They aren't definitive.

Furuyama's decades of experience, having seen free homeschooled children become successful adults, has been very valuable. He's not one to impose his opinion strongly on others, but he has told us on several occasions, "Be patient. Boys often take more time to be ready to learn these things than girls. Akira may get to his early teens before he is interested in math."

We're only a few months into his second year of homeschooling as I write, and looking back, we've made great progress nonetheless.

Akira learned to read Japanese first, and thereafter English, later than Arina. Unsurprising, given his endless energy levels and short attention span for things he isn't particularly interested in. He'd completed his phonics workbooks by the time he was seven, during his first year of primary school.

He had remained reluctant to read, so the search continued for books that interested him. I tried Enid Blyton's *Secret Seven* series, which had led me to enjoying books during my childhood and also for Arina. They didn't work.

I then asked an excellent primary school teacher in the U.K., who is also a close cousin, for advice. *Horrid Henry* books, written by Francesca Simon, proved much more enjoyable for Akira, and helped get him interested, which then led to other books as his confidence and English reading improved. It did take much less effort for him to read Japanese, which he still seems to prefer—for now…

Shortly before leaving school, during his first year Akira began to take an interest in remote-controlled toys. Taking apart a cheap R/C car, he took two small electric motors as part of the assembly, glued some small propellers from a broken drone to each motor's shaft, then used a hot-glue gun, cardboard and some scrap insulation foam to construct a boat, propelled by one motor blowing air from the back, and the other mounted at the front, which would blow to steer in either direction. As might be expected, the fragile, thin wires broke.

I took the opportunity to show him how to make a simple switch, so the batteries wouldn't go flat when not in use, and to also let him learn simple soldering, by example and practical experience of his own. He won that summer's project prize, and the toy was displayed for other students to see at his school.

Over his first year of homeschooling, still embracing and

supporting his interests in cars, planes, and boats (these are also things I have an interest in and we can therefore enjoy together), I suggested we buy a couple of inexpensive beginner's remote-controlled airplanes, which we would fly together. I made it clear that without knowing how planes fly, we'd soon crash and break them, so it was important to learn how they worked.

Being super excited at the notion of flying R/C planes together, he was keen to understand flight, so I ordered a colorful book in English for children his age all about planes, which explained how they work. Within a couple of weeks, he'd read it cover to cover. He'd understood how lift was created, what each flap would do, and what the various component parts of planes are called. When they arrived, we checked their center of gravity and flew them.

Yes—we soon managed to crash and break them… Arrgh, disaster!

Or was it?

Our mistakes led to opportunities to work out how to repair each plane, while developing our basic engineering skills and knowledge together. Akira thereby learned a little more about simple DC electrical power circuits, and soon he became a good R/C pilot. We have recently bought another small R/C plane, which has a camera on board which transmits video footage to goggles. Next, he'll be flying it as virtual reality. This is progress.

Being so interested, he also began to build and fly his own paper, cardboard, and light wood airplane designs, some of which he often excitedly showed me worked amazingly well.

In addition, he has independently researched and built a couple of simple hovercraft. We're currently awaiting the arrival of some inexpensive components before we design and build a simple remote-controlled hovercraft.

Isn't it interesting that just a seed of interest in planes led to the learning of simple physics, and engineering, English reading and vocabulary, basic planning, design and manual dexterity skills? So much knowledge can develop naturally through play.

I mentioned at the beginning Akira's untidiness, and strength in avoidance of doing things he didn't want to. I'd tried explaining to him that an engineer wouldn't be very good if he kept losing parts, or left an important component to rattle around inside an engine that could cause severe damage. He'd listen, but promptly continued to leave all sorts of unfinished projects on the kitchen table.

Venting my frustrations didn't work, I knew frustrations were my problem, not his! I tried inspiring him to help me with my own projects at work, restoring classic cars. This interested him and Furuyama San commented that Akira's engineering and understanding of how things work are advanced for his age, but I didn't really see his working on cars with me brought out much passion to help drive his continued learning and understanding. Maybe it was too early.

On his ninth birthday, a much more inspiring solution presented itself. I found an old racing go-cart on an online auction, which someone hadn't used for about 10 years, and made sure I bought it. When I confessed excitedly, a week before his birthday, that it would be delivered the next day, his enthusiasm to learn all about it, seeing an old and slightly rusty racing cart turn up, was immense!

We turned it into a shiny working driving machine, which kept him engrossed for an entire weekend, well past his bedtime. We worked together in our workshop, with music he likes playing in the background. While taking it apart, he practically understood that tools had sizes, based on mm. He quickly understood the clear importance of bagging small components and storing them safely, so we would be able to complete reassembly later.

I'd told him many times, it was important to be tidy as an engineer—and here he was, cleaning and putting tools away when finished with them, so he'd know where they were next time.

The used cart cost us $350, complete with an engine. A fraction of what they cost new. It was a non-runner that had been stored for around 10 years after the previous owner's son had grown too big for it, but was perfect for Akira to enjoy for three years or so. We spent another $150 on engine and carburetor overhaul parts. With use of a few basic tools, car cleaning supplies, lubricants, small fasteners, some information found online, and a few late evenings, we soon had it ready to use, looking very nice too!

I shared with Akira that racing go-carts were expensive things to run. There would be costs of taking the cart to and from the local racetrack, track fees, tires, safety equipment I still had to find, etc., and that for me and Yuko to invest in such would require his commitment. I really wanted him to be able to learn to drive well, but just like with R/C planes, he'd have to study how carts work and how to best drive a cart to be able to use it effectively.

There's great wealth in a shared hobby between a parent and child. Where there is an insatiable interest, the learning that is possible is immense!

In just a few evenings, Akira learned the basics of how a very simple petrol engine, steering, brakes, etc. work. He's still at the beginning and will soon come to understand how geometry of the steering mechanism affects the way his cart performs, then begin to appreciate the importance of understanding such principles of physics as conservation of momentum, coefficient of friction, etc., if he wants to drive faster.

A couple of weeks later, I was fortunate enough to befriend a retired but active go-carting racer, who upon seeing Akira's and my enthusiasm, very kindly offered to give us two old, rusty, but sound adult-sized go-carts, from which we could create one good one. He saw that by giving us his unwanted old machines he'd make it possible for me to accompany Akira on the circuit, to enjoy playing, and having fun together.

In the process, he could see, just as with his own son, we would create memories together that may be treasured by both of us for the rest of our lives. This kind man was planting seeds of passion, and thereby, possibilities for us. Akira didn't waste any time in wanting to help rebuild this one with me too!

Fast forward a further six months, and we have each replaced our carts with newer ones. We've rebuilt, perfected and sold the old carts to provide the proceeds to facilitate the purchase of better carts, aiding the evolution of our shared hobby. Akira has developed excellent driving skills that I for one am in awe of. In a day, he attended an unfamiliar race track, and by the end of the day, was lapping at speeds that other children had spent a year getting to know. Clearly, he put a lot of thought into how he could be faster.

We still have far to travel in this learning that is likely to lead to many more discoveries in future for Akira.

Soichiro Honda (founder of Honda Motor Company), also homeschooled, started out with much less, working together at his father's bicycle shop and learning blacksmith skills as a young boy. The opportunities Mr. Honda learned from were similar in playing with concepts of engineering. See, engineering development of any kind is usually a process of trial and error.

When something doesn't work, an inquisitive and interested child asks himself why, and continues to tinker until he triumphs with a solution. This is why, for a child who has a strong passion for cars, an old go-cart and the possibility of using it is a perfect gift. I know, starting at half the age I did, with much more exciting things to tinker with, he stands to learn a lot. Fast!

Now let's compare the above to an imaginary typical learning environment in the classroom. An environment where learning would be expected, accompanied by explanations and diagrams on the blackboard, possibly with some models to show such concepts as conservation of momentum.

A student of nine years old wouldn't be likely to learn quite as much, and might even get a poor grade if tested on his knowledge. If he were tested several times and was unable to get top results, would he be convinced he was no good at this subject?

Which of the above scenarios would offer a more enthralling method of learning? Tinkering with, driving, racing and understanding many different aspects of mathematics, physics, or being shown how to do simple mathematical calculations, but not use them practically—this, for a young boy who has a passion for cars!?

The answer is clear to me. How about you?

I remember once being saddened to hear from Akira when he was still only in his first year of primary school, "I'm not very smart." I asked him who'd told him that. He said, "I did," and went on to explain he wasn't good at completing the tests the teachers gave him.

I told him, "Don't ever believe you're not smart. You're super smart! You know how to make people laugh, which requires intelligence and the ability to think not just of what to say, but at the same time, in knowing what others will laugh at. A brain that is capable of that is one of intelligence. I know I don't have that ability myself, so you're actually smarter than me, Akira."

Since beginning homeschooling, we've continued to acknowledge him whenever we see something to affirm that he's smart, because we know:

WHATEVER WE BELIEVE OF OURSELVES IS WHAT WE LIVE INTO.

His studying in his first year of homeschooling unsurprisingly grew. As I write, now into his second year at home, he's been reading one of my instructional books on cart racing techniques. He wants to learn about how to control his cart better, to become faster, and how to set up his cart to run well. Step by step.

We mustn't underestimate the value in shared hobbies with our children if we're fortunate enough to enjoy the same things together. It's an opportunity for great fun, experience, bonding and fellowship and, of course, learning.

Remembering how many times over the years he's excitedly shown me his latest project, or how well a plane of his own design flies, Akira clearly seeks my approval, so I acknowledge his efforts and give him genuine praise.

Arina's hobbies in singing (Search Arina V on YouTube!), dance, ballet, drawing and jewelry making are things that Yuko is clearly much more aligned with.

Akira's ideal of a perfect day is one spent enjoying mechanical toys together with me. Arina's is to go shopping with Yuko and do girls' things together.

We naturally enjoy spending time all together too. We cook together, eat, go camping, swimming, snorkeling, hiking, and exploring places together. We continuously develop as they mature, instilling the importance of tidiness. We garden together, so they understand not just how good food is produced in harmony with nature, but its importance for health and possibly even their own homestead in future.

This autumn while Arina is still seeing her year out in Okinawa, to complement our two chickens and cockerel, we got another 16 chicks for Akira to look after into adulthood. He knows they'll start producing eggs by spring next year, and we'll have over a dozen absolutely organic and delicious free-range eggs each day. Far too much for ourselves! Akira and his sister will be able to visit various neighbors each day, and offer our eggs in return for whatever money they want to give as part of building a gift economy and creating relationships with neighbors.

Our idea is not for the children to keep the money they receive to spend on whatever they want. No; as we know they like to have spending money, this will be an opportune time for them to each create a mini business. It can be anything! For example, in making jewelry, or 3D printing discontinued but sought-after classic car parts, and offering them online.

In this way, the children can turn eggs into a little money, and from it, invest, be creative, learn new skills, and learn how to build commerce and make an income for themselves, and perhaps for our family's monthly expenses too. They also learn responsibility through caring for animals, and these are beautiful (Plymouth rock) chickens, a gentle breed.

Gaining such knowledge at a young age, while building one's own self-confidence in being able to create prosperity, is another valuable homeschooling step which they certainly don't teach at school, but should!

Another avenue for fun and learning together, and a means by which they'll gain skills that may serve them well for their lives ahead. If we can show our children how to build abundance of financial means at a young age, they'll know they're capable of doing so once they're adults. I anticipate and hope they may create other ventures too. Sometimes, we just need to plant a seed for children to run wild with.

Yuko and I share our affection for one another openly in front of the kids, so they naturally absorb what a healthy relationship is, and begin to make their own blueprint for what they may want for themselves. Perhaps more importantly, we hope they'll get a basic sense of relationships to avoid getting involved in that may not be worthwhile.

We make sure we have interesting conversations to discuss and plan together where it's important to build skills and eloquence in speech. We always share with the children knowledge of the world, including geopolitical issues, so they have a good basic grasp of world knowledge upon which to build their own wisdom.

So you see, free homeschooling is not only about learning academically, but offers a rich wealth of so much more. It's about development of relationship skills for each of the family, while doing things that inspire and excite us. It's about enjoyment. It's about growth of children's confidence and self-belief. It's about encouraging and equipping children to become the greatest people they are inspired to be. It's about understanding and sharing what love is.

Choice is a wonderfully empowering thing and we are in the fortunate position to be able to offer our children and others who visit our home the possibility to learn naturally through choices of varied learning activities. We intend to continue to expand choices of activities for children as resources allow, and we thank and acknowledge those who have helped us create, build, learn together, and build the local homeschooling community, while participating in activities.

To finish this chapter, I would add that we have always remained in contact with the primary school, while maintaining a good relationship. To maintain a good relationship with schools is beneficial, as the staff are doing the best they are able to for children, while having to conduct themselves within often difficult guidelines, often with insufficient funding, understaffing, and other difficulties.

The teachers at our local school are aware we are not just letting our children sit in front of a TV, spend their day playing computer games, or be addicted to social media. They know we are intent on homeschooling children as well as we possibly can, and are in turn as supportive as they can be.

Just this week, Akira's schoolteacher dropped by to give him more worksheets. By coincidence, she came on the day we had homeschooled children and their mothers as our guests, playing and learning together. The teacher was taken by the hand by one of the girls and shown the project they'd been working on. She saw the smiles and delight in their faces and commented that Akira looked so happy and content. She mentioned his demeanor had been different and not as positive when he had attended school.

No doubt, teachers see the differences and are inspired. Sadly, they don't have the freedom to develop more inspiring methods of learning, in an environment where results must be quantitative, monitored, and recorded through testing.

We have no problems at all with the local government authorities, and teachers are welcome to see our progress.

Rules and laws may be different for your country, so we would naturally recommend checking and satisfying yourself that it would be legal to homeschool where you live, if considering removing your child from his current school.

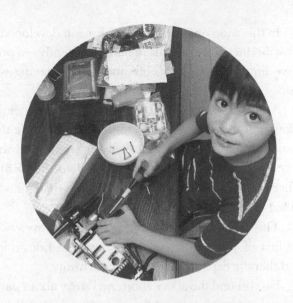

5 What Makes Children Smart

Thomas Edison[1] started his homeschooling just two-and-a-half months after enrolling at school when he was no longer allowed to attend due to being a hyperactive child prone to distraction. When he asked his mother what the teacher's letter had said, she told him he had been sent home because he was too smart to be at school.

Edison spent the next couple of years learning by himself as the youngest of seven children. By the time he was 11, Thomas had developed a voracious appetite for knowledge, reading books on a wide range of subjects.

In this wide-open curriculum, Edison developed his own process for self-education and learning independently—a process that would serve him throughout his life and where playing was a part of his work.

At just 12 years old, Edison managed to convince his parents to allow him to sell newspapers to passengers along the Grand Trunk Railroad line, near where they lived. Taking advantage of having access to the news bulletins teletyped to the local railway station office each day, Edison launched his own small newspaper, which he called the Grand Trunk Herald.

This newspaper proved popular with travelers. This was to be his first of many business ventures where Edison identified a need and thereby capitalized on the opportunity.

Do you find the above shortened story about part of Edison's life to be thought provoking? Imagine the simple yet harder life he, his family and community must have lived. Picture what life could have been like for this disruptive, distracted and hyperactive young child who'd had a hearing impairment through suffering from an early bout of scarlet fever, back in in the mid-1800s.

Clearly, his parents weren't people of wealth, nor were they likely to have had much time to spend with him when they would have had to share time with all his siblings too. He'd have had more companionship from his siblings when they weren't at school.

Thomas Edison later remembered: *"My mother was the making of me. She was so true, so sure of me; and I felt I had something to live for, someone I must not disappoint."*

How incredible to picture that even in such times he'd developed a voracious appetite for knowledge some years after being disallowed from attending school. Like all children of the time, he wouldn't have had as many toys as children of today, but instead would have had to make his own. Later, he would use old junk, basic materials and commonly available chemicals to experiment and make things with.

In spite of the many difficulties he faced, compared to what even some of the children from the least privileged families have today, he was able to progress greatly, through his own determination to fulfil his desires.

He'd learned to read late, as the earliest he'd have spent his three months of school would have been as a seven-year-old. Having some hearing difficulties, he wouldn't have been likely to have used his hearing as a primary sense for learning; indeed, he would have been unlikely to have been a great listener.

To have had a voracious appetite for knowledge, he'd have needed resourcefulness. It's unlikely Edison would have had a great choice of books to choose from at a library, even if there had been any library at all. Then, aged just 12, he'd somehow put together all the means with which to print news, along with all the logistical effort this would have entailed. A fascinating scenario to imagine, yet alone to live in and, above all, to grow and triumph from.

By the end of his life, Edison had patented over 1,000 inventions and his estate's value exceeded $12 million, which was so much wealth back then that by today the figure would be closer to 10 times that.

It's interesting to follow the family progression of Thomas Edison from birth to death and beyond, and how his existence touched and made a difference to the lives of so many. Today, there is still an Edison Innovation Foundation to be found in New Jersey, U.S.A.

I look at our son aged eight and see similarities in several ways. He already speaks and reads two languages. He has lots of natural knowledge, albeit only a small proportion of which he gleaned from his classes before choosing to start homeschooling. Through his own interests, he can already tell me much more than I have ever learned about insects and crustaceans.

He, like so many natural children today, was sometimes distracted and very energetic, unable to sit still in class, before he started homeschooling. I look back at myself as a child and recall how I'd always been energetic and how I was easily distracted and prone to daydreaming in my younger years too. Such memories, though, remind me of how valuable those years were, even though I hadn't been fully paying attention to what the teachers were trying to instill in me.

Voracious readers are often people who had a lot of stories read to them before they could read themselves, starting at a time when their imaginations were most vivid. Parents sow seeds for progress when reading bedtime stories. The children whose parents continue to read to them even once the children can read themselves most certainly continue to benefit. Children can absorb many of the gains that come from hearing and understanding (through context) new words, eloquence of the spoken word, and exercising of the imagination, to name but just a few.

As I look back through life, the people I have met as the most knowledgeable, inspiring and memorable are those who have been "well read." These are people who as young children developed their own fascination with books and today relax and take pleasure in becoming absorbed in the contents of publications containing new knowledge or stories.

I wonder if, like I do, you remember visiting some people's homes and marveled at their collection of wonderful books on rows upon rows of shelves. The smell of a library of books and the eloquence and wisdom with which a well-read person often speaks. How much knowledge can a person who finds comfort in reading amass over a lifetime?

Home libraries and their content can tell a lot about a person, and of course looking only at the covers, perhaps even having read a few of the titles we spot, we would still be only seeing the briefest fleeting glimpse of their reading experiences.

BOOKS ARE THE SEEDS PREPARED BY OTHERS FOR THE GROWTH OF OUR KNOWLEDGE.

Often, we will find the wisest people we meet have since childhood read many books throughout the years. They also tend to be the most eloquent in their choices of words, having built a greater volume of vocabulary.

Physical books are often available in libraries, but sadly since the widescale adoption of computers, then the internet and now smartphones, the trend is dying, and public libraries are slowly disappearing.

For many young children, literature now comes from internet sources, and for many along the way, books are in danger of becoming unloved, borrowed indefinitely, lost, or discarded.

The internet and hand-held devices carry grave dangers of distraction for children, but many parents don't appreciate the dangers (to be presented and discussed separately, in sub-chapter The Digital Pacifier). This and many others reinforce strong justification for us as conscious parents to encourage an early love for books for children.

The reading of books for themselves clearly allows children to exercise and continue to develop their imaginations. Let's stop for a moment and consider some of what they can absorb.

As children continue to read further, they stand to naturally develop not just their vocabulary, punctuation, grammar, and spelling, but writing style, articulation and last, but clearly not least, the potential for an ever greater depth of knowledge.

As we each develop our reading, seeds for knowledge are continuously planted, sprouting more questions and a yearning for answers.

As they grow each year, children may thereby be increasingly likely to come to find their opinions formed as being deeper, better formed, and more interesting than many who don't read nearly as much.

We may find ourselves enjoying contemplating ideas together as we progress through conversations with them.

Edison's story and so many others you will undoubtedly come across may also serve to remind us that we must be patient. We must avoid pushing or nagging our child to improve his reading, but rather inspire him continuously through fun means. If one book or a collection doesn't work, be patient and try another.

We may also be trying too early. In his own time, he'll discover for himself that reading and absorbing new knowledge will open doors to an infinite world of discoveries. Enchantment comes from learning new things and going on to create more, as and when he is inspired.

Looking back, I remember poring over maps when I was younger with an interest in learning where the subjects of stories were from and what their lives might have been like, their climates, the cultures, and more.

Using animated books and subjects we see he's fascinated with, our now nine-year-old son has been developing steadily. Some years prior to that, our daughter became a voracious reader in two languages herself.

After performing poorly in a traditional one-room schoolhouse, Thomas Edison's mother refused to believe the teacher's assessment that young Thomas's "brains were addled." His teacher wrote to Nancy and said Thomas couldn't attend school anymore as he was too disruptive. When Thomas asked his mother what the letter contained, she told him the teacher had said he was too intelligent to be at school and that he should learn at home.

Clearly Thomas was experiencing the world quite differently from his classmates. Through her commitment to nurturing and leadership, she instilled in him the basic tools to learn, while supplying him with the basic materials and facilities to study and play.

Thomas did so, learning that failure was an opportunity to learn. He became a voracious reader over a wide span of topics, while also learning through playing with things practically. With a self-imbued passion for learning, he never stopped absorbing knowledge and went on to discover and invent many great things, notably the phonograph and the development of incandescent light bulbs that could last for over 1,000 hours (contrary to popular belief he wasn't the inventor of the light bulb). He also invented the motion picture camera and the alkaline battery.

In all, Thomas Edison went on to register a total of a staggering 1,093 patents successfully during his career.

"To invent, you need a good imagination and a pile of junk."

"I never did a day's work in my life. It was all fun."

- THOMAS EDISON

https://www.edisonmuckers.org

Was Thomas Edison's teacher right in saying "his brains were addled?"

Another very important aspect of bringing up strongly able and smart kids is of course progress. In turn, for children (and adults) to make continual meaningful progress, it's vital they have strength in self-belief and commitment.

One of my favorite quotes by Henry Ford is:

"Whether you believe you can do it, or whether you believe you cannot, either way, you're absolutely right."

Another is:

"Obstacles are those frightful things you see when you take your eyes off your goals."

Although it's important to help our children develop and demonstrate how to achieve their intentions, for example by showing them tools and thereby widening their scope of possibility, on the flipside it's important to avoid shutting it down. One aspect of modern schooling in Japan that we noticed was the propensity to test children at a young age. Although tests can guide the teacher in knowing where a child may be lacking in learning a part of a given curriculum, what can the costs of testing be for a young and easily impressionable child?

In the context of Henry Ford's quotations above,[2] if a child continuously gets bad results in his early math tests, is there not a danger that child will come to believe she doesn't have an aptitude for this work when possibly she just wasn't inspired? I would question if the danger may be an unfair and disempowering way of learning, where possibility can be shut down on a permanent basis for many children.

In the previous chapter, we looked at two very different examples of how a child can learn, with the example given of Akira's go-carting know-how, and how one method of learning is so much more passion inspiring than the other.

We also looked at how he had been led to believe he wasn't very smart, as a result of not having top scores in his tests (in particular with Japanese writing when he was learning two languages and not one!); and we looked at how it is beneficial to understand and believe in the possibility to enhance and continuous development of one's abilities.[3]

For example, if, say, our young child was, perhaps with a group of other children, actively measuring and cutting pieces of wood to create walls for a small roofed building, which would have an upside down V-shaped roof, windows, door and a raised floor, the children would be using basic arithmetic for addition, subtraction, multiplication, geometry and even simple fractions. Would a child who may have not done well in a quiet test in a classroom have necessarily been just as disinterested at working with other children on a project such as this?

The best form of learning and forming of understanding is when any of us immediately use knowledge we are gaining in the process of doing something practical. Not least, if children are especially enjoying the activity at hand, then they're a lot more likely to want to continue to do more, and thereby learn further.

Some might say that the best teacher is not one who insists on children being instructed on specifically what to learn, but one who provides the materials, facilities, freedom and seeds of inspiration for children to explore and from which to absorb knowledge. It's a big leap of faith for some, but having seen this at work, Yuko and I, and of course our kids, continue to move ever closer to this mindset.

Another well-known homeschooler, and as a car enthusiast myself, a fascinating personal hero of mine is the Japanese industrialist and engineer Soichiro Honda. A remarkable achiever who learned much from practical activities, and just look at what he achieved in his lifetime!

Soichiro grew up near Hamamatsu, where later he'd set up his main Honda factory.[4]

Helping in his father's small business repairing bicycles, while working as a blacksmith, he famously forged his family's name stamp to falsify his attendance at school, before making them for other children. He borrowed his father's bicycle to attend a demonstration of an airplane, where he first began to develop his love for engines and engineering.

At 15, with no formal education, he traveled to Tokyo to begin work as a car mechanic.

In 1937, aged 31, he founded Tōkai Seiki, a company making piston rings for Toyota, which was destroyed in 1944 during the course of World War II. He sold the remains for ¥450,000 before continuing relentlessly in pursuit of what he was focused on: inventing what he was passionate about.

In 1948, Soichiro established Honda Motor Company Ltd., where he began manufacturing small engines for fitment to bicycles. From there, he progressed continuously, first with making many great leaps in the development of motorcycles and engines, then in 1963 with the domestic (Japanese) market T360 pickup truck. Thereafter, marked by a great many historic steps in racing and manufacturing, Honda became the name that millions around the world today hold as their favorite car and motorcycle manufacturer.

Some say Soichiro Honda had no formal education. He lived with basic opportunities to learn about the things he grew passions for. Many other homeschoolers have similarly been able to achieve great things through their passions.

By the time he was retired, Soichiro and his wife Satchi were also both accomplished private pilots. Soichiro enjoyed racing cars, skiing, golf, hang-gliding, and hot-air ballooning.

He was a man who followed his dreams throughout life. A great inspiration for many including myself. Together with our son Akira, I have rebuilt a beautiful modern classic car in tribute to this great man, and intend to create another soon as part of his homeschooling, if he is suitably inspired.

THE EARLY LEARNING OF LANGUAGES.

Children who learn second languages at an early stage create more neurological links in their minds, which helps in the enhancement intelligence.[5]

Children who learn two languages at the same time, although often later to speak confidently, have more developed problem-solving abilities and creativity, and, at least in these times before AI develops further, will have greater career opportunities in adulthood. They also naturally find it easier to connect with other cultures, which makes them more open-minded and tolerant of diversity.

It's been observed that children who learn a second language when very young grow up to be expert problem solvers and creative thinkers, where their brains experience more intensive activity. The brain is something which must be used in order to remain sharp— and some say later in life, with multiple language use, we are less likely to experience age-related mental illness.

IF A BOOK IS A DREAM THAT YOU HOLD IN YOUR HANDS, THEN MUSIC IS HOW WE PAINT TIME.

Both of our children thankfully enjoy music.

Watching Arina as a baby, we could see how much she enjoyed singing and dancing; it seems only natural she has retained a passion for music and is committed to becoming a professional vocalist in future.

Although he showed no interest in musical play during kindergarten, and his interest in learning to play the guitar was short lived, this year Akira declared he really wanted to learn to play the drums. Still a little over energetic, we figured it would be good if he did learn the drums, and of course, develop musical rhythm.

So I searched for and found a broken Roland electric drum set online, and bought it last winter. Knowing it was a simple device, together we dismantled the offending pedals, found two broken rubber parts, ordered replacements online, and repaired it, upon which Akira began to learn by himself.

We were kindly introduced to a younger family (by Akira's schoolteacher) whose father is a drum enthusiast. Our son gets an occasional drum lesson, and also continues learning well by himself. We often hear him drumming in harmony with his favorite tunes, and although we can hear mistakes, he continues to strive for perfection and improvement. He seems to favor rock and is developing his tastes for bands he has listened to with me, say when traveling in a car together.

At a recent jazz event where his sister was invited to sing, he desperately wanted to play the drums, and the band kindly allowed him to make his debut. He has far to go, but we see the enthusiasm in his eyes.

This is an example of how we as parents can provide the materials and facilitate our children's learning with what they have a passion for.

Music, if they have an interest in it, is especially important. Scientific research has shown that musical training is associated with improved perceptual and cognitive skills, including executive functions and general intelligence, particularly in childhood. Memorization of musical sequences, tones and rhythms exercises the mind, and builds links in the brain. If we observe, we find that the most gifted and talented musicians we encounter in life are often people of intelligence.[6]

TRAVEL BROADENS THE MIND. THERE IS NO SUBSTITUTE FOR EXPERIENCE.

Many of us have heard these phrases, although many still haven't experienced the magic of traveling afar for themselves. Sadly, the freedom to fly to other countries has been made more difficult in our lifetimes now than ever before, but we must live in the hope that humanity will prevail and the adventure and learning that is possible through international travel will resume someday.

In many countries, there is still freedom to travel by land and so much to see. Never give up—there are a great many discovery opportunities closer than you may think. Explore them!

Traveling helps us realize how much more there can be to life than the routines into which we live day-to-day. It instills a natural interest in geography, as children explore and discover there are so many different places they want to see for themselves.

When we are fortunate enough to enjoy traveling experiences and meeting others, for example, in seeing and partly experiencing the lives of children in Third World countries, our children may also be able to learn empathy and compassion, while realizing and appreciating how blessed our lives are. These experiences can help instill wisdom that may be difficult to share with our children otherwise.

Especially for those who live in cities, traveling enables us to see and learn to appreciate the serenity and wisdom that exists in natural beauty. We may also see for ourselves the destruction of nature that is accelerating on a global scale, even during the strange times we currently live in, and to think of the world we may leave behind for our children to live into, and for them and us to see for ourselves and begin to contemplate the urgency of doing what we can to improve life for humanity as a whole.

There is no limit to how much can be learned in nature, and from a perspective of sustainability, children may be delighted to know that there is no such thing as waste in a natural system.

Everything nature produces has a purpose and a use. Even weeds perform important tasks, also telling us a lot about what is happening in a particular area of our environment, if we absorb an understanding of them.

Being around nature is a natural way of learning wisdom and the study of life (also known as biology). Planting seeds and saplings and witnessing their growth, rearing small animals and seeing how they interact with nature, becoming accustomed to insects and wildlife are all fun experiences we have seen our two children learn a great deal from, while living surrounded by natural beauty and during our times spent traveling together.

WITHOUT KNOWING TRUTH, WE ARE POWERLESS TO CREATE CHANGE FOR THE BETTER.

Yuko and I believe it is important to be as open and honest about life, what we know and believe, and to be the best examples we can be for others, as possible. We have shared knowledge with our kids since they learned to speak. This has included wars fought in the world, as much as possible from both sides.

We live in a world where the narrative is often one-sided, and most just believe it, without making an effort to understand what the other side is experiencing. So we studied subjects such as the Syrian war and what the financial goals may be, since who seeks control of wealth is often the indicator of where the real reasons behind the investment it takes for wars to be fought.

We share what we see is happening in these Coronavirus times; the sad loss of ability for people to build new relationships around themselves and what the possible ongoing measures may be, while avoiding speculating too much on wild theories.

We look at the human costs and overall deaths to form an independent understanding of the costs of measures being taken, then discuss what we can do to help others understand what is being lost, without making them wrong for having a difference of opinion from that which we may form. After all, believing in false hopes can be as disempowering to the self as believing in lies. Truth is important to understand and to seek.

We have interesting conversations at every meal and where there is an opportunity to spend time together conversation flows. We aim to talk about things we are passionate about, to draw out emotion and interest in the conversation. Communication and the ability to convey language well is an important aspect of being smart—otherwise, what good is understanding if we are unable to effectively express ourselves?

LOVE IS THE MOST POWERFUL FORCE OF ALL AND HOW WE EXEMPLIFY IT IS THE GREATEST WAY TO INFLUENCE OTHERS.

If we ask people what the definition of love is, few can give a clear answer, even though the fortunate ones among us have felt it and the most blessed live with it in their lives.

The best and simplest definition of love that I have come across:

"Love is the complete acceptance of another, without condition."[7]

Yuko and I are blessed to have always aligned strongly as a couple. We honor, serve and accept one another fully, and we aim to be the best example of a couple to our children, so they in turn are familiar with what force of good a strongly committed, loving couple can empower one another and their family with. I acknowledge every day how beautiful she is to me, not just physically, but the person she is, and how she strengthens me.

We have had big challenges in our lives together and probably will going forward, but I feel an unshakable sense of peace in knowing that she is always by my side, ready to support me, and in turn she knows I'll always be there, supporting and listening to her.

We observe our children are developing their own similar understanding of what a good family is, and how important it is as a grounding. We have the power of love in our family, and observe it can be infectious to others we meet.

If we give without expectation of others, the greatest things come to us naturally. This can be facilitated in a confidence and belief in oneself that can come from an environment in which we grow up surrounded in love. This is why my friend Ann, who together with her husband Alex homeschooled 10 of her own children, was so right in saying to me and Yuko, months after we were married when we visited them in Cambodia:

"Marinate your children daily in love, so that when they grow up, they'll be really juicy."

We wish love for all of humanity, and this is the overbearing emotion we carry in sharing this book and what we know with all of you.

CURRICULUM

—

6 How to Homeschool

"We only have one future, and it will be made of our dreams, if we have the courage to challenge convention."

– SOICHIRO HONDA

Public school teachers may do their utmost to persuade us and our children that the right thing to do is to attend school. They may try to entice them with the activities our children enjoy most.

Traditionalists may say that homeschooling is not rigorous enough without following national curriculum textbooks and ever more frequent test-taking. Have these traditionalists much experience of seeing children's learning rates when it is through what they're passionate about?

Having the benefit of meeting other like-minded homeschooling parents is a good way to set our perceived reality. At first, Yuko and I were apprehensive of homeschooling and our own abilities. One of our best moves was to join a small association of natural homeschooler parents and children, where we could ask questions and observe children of all ages. There, we met children with passions they'd developed by themselves that in turn would inspire us further. Now, we've met many more, not least through seeing the continuous development of our son and daughter.

Free homeschooling is not the home equivalent of conventional schooling. Seeking to recreate a school curriculum for children to learn the same subjects from the same textbooks while at home would be tragically overlooking the opportunities that await when we as parents awake and realize the abundance of learning wealth that becomes possible through a change of perspective.

We have covered some of this in the sub-chapter What is Free Homeschooling, where I gave examples of children's activities, and how they learn naturally while playing and enjoying time, but still one of the most common questions about free homeschooling from parents who haven't yet experienced homeschooling their kids is, "What is the curriculum?"

Of course you know by now—there simply isn't one, and nor should there be. We must give up the notion that with education one size fits all. Each child has individual interests that resonate and become relevant at different periods of their development. Learning is most effective whenever new knowledge is used simultaneously.

The possible activities individual children can do while learning are infinite, and bound only by our and their imaginations. Yes, if they respond well to them, by all means use workbooks. Indeed, this is one method we employ ourselves, so children learn the basics. For example: phonics, for learning to read English, or basic arithmetic workbooks, but whenever possible, we remind them of where they use such knowledge. Workbooks are just one method of learning, and are quite possibly not the most effective way.

The main challenge Yuko and I have had to overcome has been where we catch ourselves (or not, as the case may be!) comparing our children's perceived knowledge to that of children who go to school, or how advanced our own academic education was at their ages, then telling them their learning is not fast enough and that they must catch up. If we look deeper though, homeschoolers can learn so much more than schoolchildren. Learning which will serve their futures far better than today's conventional schooling.

So aim to catch and stop yourselves if you encounter a problem. If your children are not paying attention to something, it is often because they're more inspired by something else, or repelled by the methods we are trying to employ. As it's our job to support, we can look into ways to make their learning of a particular subject more interesting, inspiring, and **fun**!

Interest in almost anything may be important for the individual. **How** it is presented also plays a very important aspect of an individual's learning.

THE VARK® MODEL OF LEARNING

Due to copyright rules, we would be unable to print VARK® information, so please visit their website directly: https://vark-learn.com/the-vark-questionnaire/

The questionnaire on this website will help you and your child work out by which method(s) and senses they learn most effectively. We differ from one another.

You may already have noticed that your child has a particularly favored form of learning, or a sense which may be stronger than others, which he uses most. This is not to say that we should concentrate solely on the category they most favor, all should be employed and developed as much as possible—especially through enjoyable activities—but I would say that in general one of the four categories is more resonant than the others for each of us. Where it works best, make use!

The VARK® system is used to describe four distinct categories through which a student learns. These categories were identified in a 1992 study by Neil D. Fleming and Coleen E. Mills.

VARK® is short for the four different categories of:

Visual, Auditory, Reading/Writing and Kinesthetic.

These categories were identified following thousands of hours of observation into how students individually absorbed information most effectively. The study led to a questionnaire being optimized for educators, to help them identify and understand a student's learning preferences.

VISUAL LEARNERS

Those children who most readily absorb information when it's presented to them in a graphic depiction. This can be in the form of pictures, symbols, and watching to gain an understanding of how a task is resolved.

Visual learners process information best when it's presented to them as a robust whole, rather than piecemeal. In other words, some children learn best when something is presented within a whole picture, rather than many pages and pictures of information in one go.

This isn't to say that videos don't work for visual learners. I myself find that my strongest memories and learning have been formed visually. Some visual learners can be observed to have a stronger photographic memory than most.

Akira has a strong penchant for visual learning and is clearly to be found more absorbed in books with diagrams and colorful pictures. He learns from making or tinkering with things. Clues like this give us parents a guide, but are not always conclusive, which is why it's also useful to use the VARK questionnaire, link available above.

AUDITORY LEARNERS

Auditory (or aural) learners are most likely to be able to recall things they hear from the spoken word. Children with this learning style may tend not to make notes or highlight important key points in a book during times of study. This can be to best maintain their unbroken auditory attention.

Children who fall into this modality often find success in activities where we ask them to discuss what they learned with us, as we invoke increasingly detailed questions of today's activities. They may also benefit from reading their studies aloud to themselves.

Arina, as an example, has always especially been more inspired by music, and in her leisure time likes to play the piano and sing as she studies. Clues such as this can give a guide but are not conclusive. Again, use the VARK® questionnaire with your children, while observing how they best respond.

READING / WRITING LEARNERS

Children who benefit best from reading/writing tend to have a stronger affinity for the written word. They're the most likely (but clearly not the only ones) to enjoy a day with their heads buried in a good book.

PowerPoint slide presentations of online courses, as well as the opportunity to write notes while studying, is clearly beneficial for children who fall within this category. Searching online and reading about what they discover may also be favorable. If they're also logically minded, they may be more likely than others to enjoy learning computer programing.

Reading/writing-oriented students should be encouraged to use notebooks and to write journals, so they can review information they learn and have an easier time recalling it later, as needed.

KINESTHETIC LEARNERS

Kinesthetic children are hands-on and may prefer to take a physically active role in their learning processes. They're "tactile learners" but this can be a something of a misnomer.

Kinesthetic learners tend to use all their senses for learning and may be described as individuals who like to "make" things with their hands.

Because of their active nature, kinesthetic learners often have the most difficult time succeeding in conventional classroom settings where they'd have to sit still and follow what they're directed to look at while listening to instruction.

Kinesthetic children may respond better to flashcards when learning subjects such as mathematics and English, and doing role-play, such as acting in plays where they need to memorize words. These children may thrive while doing scientific practical experiments and simply tinkering.

Akira would, in my observations, fall most within this category, even though he also learns well visually. From my observations of our son, this is why I am inclined to let him learn through playing with insects, small animals, mechanical and electrical things, and taking things apart to make others.

IS IT POSSIBLE FOR A LEARNER TO BE IN MORE THAN ONE CATEGORY?

Few things in life are black or white, and learning preferences are no exception. Studies estimated that between 50% and 70% of people have affinities to several different styles of learning. "Multimodal Learners" tend to adapt relatively easily to typical classroom settings that engage through the use of multiple learning styles.

Just because our children may be adaptable to different learning styles does not necessarily mean that we should take the easy online video option and thereby use more than one on most occasions. Try to encourage your son to concentrate on the one he most favors.

The modern media-rich environment in front of a screen has made multi-mode learning much more accessible than ever before, but we should be mindful of excessive exposure to video screens when studying, since this may invite all sorts of other undesirable effects, such as an addiction to watching YouTube videos and playing games.

GREATEST MOTIVATIONS ARE LED BY EMOTIONS.

When we stop to ponder and really think about it, we may come to the realization that many of our own most important decisions through life have been led by emotions. Indeed, you may come to the same realization as I have, that we are very much led by the emotions we experience.

Unforgettable events during our early childhoods, most often involving our parents and siblings, are likely to include memories of an emotional response we experienced. Indeed, we are inspired by memories of extreme excitement, or getting goose bumps.

Often, the friends we choose as the most valuable are those who have and continue to make us feel the most special (including, for some, our parents).

How we may gain an important job is often about how our employer feels about us.

Without necessarily realizing it, our paths through life are mapped with emotional responses to events and often these can dictate how we choose our route, from infancy, through adolescence, and the entirety of our adult lives.[8]

Our emotions play vitally important parts in the decisions we make.

During important life-events, people most remember us not by what we said or did, but by how we have made them feel.

Plutchik's Wheel of Emotions

Due to copyright rules, we would be unable to print Plutchik's diagram here. Please visit this website directly, where you'll be able to get the diagram and its explanation of content:

https://www.6seconds.org/2020/08/11/plutchik-wheel-emotions/

Human learning is greatly affected by how we feel, so if our children feel joy while learning, this can help them to embrace and retain memories.

Psychologist Robert Plutchik created the Plutchik Model. The model shows the eight basic emotions: Joy, Trust, Fear, Surprise, Sadness, Disgust, Anger, and Anticipation.[9]

Of course, we also experience a mix of emotions, such as anger and disgust, but for the sake of simplicity in this context, we can consider that for a primary emotion that we can experience there is an opposite.

The further outward we go on the diagram, the less intense the emotion.

Sadness opposes Joy
Connection v Withdrawal
Fear opposes Anger
Get Small and Hide v Visible Anger
Anticipation opposes Surprise
Inquisitiveness v Fright
Disgust opposes Trust
Rejection v Embracing

Being immersed with bringing up our own children, and of course being a part of the many emotions that are a natural part of parenting, we often unconsciously get emotionally involved ourselves.

Similarly, as a child realizes that we make decisions through the emotions that we experience, as he grows up he may come to realize how to use this to improve the relationships he cultivates, using the power to create positive emotions.

Much time during our lives is accumulatively but unconsciously spent learning how to create opportunities for emotional responses. Few of us are acutely aware of the process and the choices made through them. For all of us, emotions are a sometimes-delightful ingredient of life.

A child may really enjoy music or a hobby precisely because of the emotional reaction she gets from a stimulus, such as the pleasing sound of a piano.

Another may really enjoy tinkering with and then driving a motorized vehicle, from which he feels triumph and elation as a reward.

Another may experience elation at triumphing in achieving a physically challenging goal, such as making a simple, small building.

It's not to say that as parents of free homeschooled children our job would be to always facilitate or create such experiences. In many cases, the children can learn while getting on with such discoveries they pick up by themselves. All through having fun and experiencing great emotions.

One of the most valuable lessons I've picked up in life that I'd like to share, and which I apply to my life and how I relate to others is this:

People remember us not for what we do, not for what we say, but how we make them feel.

I had an emotional experience last summer that I'd like to share: Akira always enjoys the experience of spending time together, so one night, he told me to wake him up at 6:30 am so he'd accompany me on my exercise bicycle ride around the countryside. Being just eight years old, he would slow me down, but I felt this experience might be worthwhile for both of us. Not least, I count myself very blessed to have a son who is prepared to do whatever it takes to spend time together doing "boys' stuff."

So, this being the height of Japan's hot and sticky summer, off we set as the sun was still low. Right from the start, he was keen. On the hills I could see he was really trying hard. A few years prior, he'd have stopped and pushed the bike up hills, but here he was still making an effort to just keep on cranking those pedals, to stay with me as much as he could!

About 40 minutes into the ride, while waiting at the top of a hill for him, I asked, "How are you feeling?"

"Sick," he said.

"Where?" I asked.

"In my stomach."

I told him I was proud of him and how hard he was working to keep up, even though it made him feel a little queasy! I also said that now he knew he could achieve a difficult challenge, because he just wouldn't give up till the job was done, even if it made him feel a little uncomfortable.

"So great!" I told him, giving him a big smile.

He didn't stop once thereafter for the remainder of the entire ride, even making it up the steepest, longest hill on top of which is our home. The end result was that we each felt joy at the end having achieved what we weren't sure we would when we'd set off an hour earlier. We each rewarded ourselves with a nice cold shower to cool off after the ride in the searing morning heat of summer.

I asked him afterward, "Would you like to join me tomorrow?" to which he replied, "No," so I said that anytime he'd like to join me, I'd always love to be accompanied by him, but I wouldn't wake him up till he asks me to.

Although it would be possible to wake him up early tomorrow and tell him we're going on a ride, it'll be much better if he joins me because he knows he can and really wants to. To impose my will on him might risk breaking down his trust. Instead, I will just continue to plant seeds and keep mentioning that in the morning I'm going for a bicycle ride. I have no doubt he'll join me again and things will develop from there.

After we'd finished our showers and gotten dressed, he asked me if I'd cycled much with my own father. I told him the truth (I hadn't). He then kept digging for more and learned that when I was younger, I used to run long distances and was fast for my age.

I could almost hear his mind ticking, thinking of what it would be like to run the same distance we'd ridden, so as he grows up, he can become like me. A lot better, is my hope, but one step at a time.

For every opportunity I want to inspire him with doing great things together and creating great memories. I want to continue to share great knowledge of things that I feel he'll become passionate about, while we continue to create these unforgettable moments with one another. Whether that be making models, riding motorcycles, tinkering with things in the workshop, racing our go-carts together, playing with critters, jumping into lakes, or any other activity. We only have a limited amount of time to enjoy a childhood together, and every day is one to be treasured as I watch him grow up.

Funnily enough, I know our daughter won't ever join me for a morning ride, or even a jog. She's just not that way inclined. It would invite annoyance and possibly anger from Arina at me having imposed my will on her, where through choice, Akira had experienced serenity and joy.

So, by the same token, I need to be mindfully aware not to impose annoyance, or loss of trust from each of our children, so their emotions and memories may be as positively instilled as possible.

Some years ago, when first homeschooling our daughter, I recall I was a lot less graceful. Being an artistic type, she didn't really see the point in doing mathematics drills (even though she's very good at math!). I realize now this was because we weren't offering her ways to use these skills in practical ways. I'd push her, making sure she did the requisite to keep up with her classmates at school. She'd protest at first, but eventually realized this is what would be required for homeschooling, and just got on with it.

Furuyama San mentioned this analogy, which applied well to our children. It may work for yours:

"Girls, especially in their younger years, tend to be adaptable and easier to persuade to become obedient."

"Boys are like cactus. They tend to want to concentrate on one subject and really get to grips with it. Once their learning is complete, they leave that lobe of cactus and begin another, unrelated study until that too is completed and then they move on to another, and so forth."

This may help explain why girls tend to speak earlier than boys during infancy, but also mature faster than boys. Boys tend to be more likely to really concentrate on one subject and become especially good. Of course, there are exceptions and these are not hard and fast rules, just an analogy, but I hope it helps you, as it did me.

Somehow, while learning the many different aspects associated with a particular subject, whether it be primarily scientific, literary or artistic, boys can and do learn many different things while studying a particular theme.

Furuyama San shared how his nephew, who was homeschooled, was very enthusiastic about skateboarding. He'd tune his board with high-speed wheels and axles that helped the board to turn more effectively. He had really studied this hobby as a subject, while developing his cactus form of learning.

Thereafter, as he completed his learning, he became very

interested in Quantum Theory and ravenously studied it.

He went on to study physics at university and today he's a respected engineer, working professionally in a well-known multinational corporation. While being homeschooled, he was not forced to study what he didn't want to, but instead encouraged to learn through what he was most interested in.

When you find yourself observing and doubting that freedom enables your child to learn naturally, ask yourself what it is he's doing at that very moment.

Look at **Plutchik's Wheel of Emotions.** How is your child learning?

If you feel she isn't progressing, ask yourself how you can better inspire her learning. What facilities does she really have a hunger for, and how would having such facilities inspire discovery and joy?

The main challenge that comes up again and again for us is where we see our children wasting time, procrastinating and not furthering their knowledge day after day. Truth—this is what happens in reality at school, only there they have much less freedom to do something they're more inspired to do.

In times such as these, we need to ask ourselves what inspires us most and empowers our child, before asking gently: Where would she find more enthusiasm in learning this subject? Could it be practically, or through reading, or absorbing the contents of a video? Is he ready to learn this, or am I trying too early?

Sometimes, being inventive offers better ways to help our children learn, and thereby breakthroughs are made.

For example, in our son's case and his love for his go-cart, he learns how many turns an eight-tooth front sprocket has to make in order to turn an 80-toothed rear sprocket, and what the maximum revs of his motor is. From these figures, he can work out how fast he'll be going at given revs, or say his top speed, at the end of the main straight on the track. Children interested in cars and how they work would probably find this particularly interesting.

For our daughter, she can work out how many biscuits she can make, knowing a given weight of cookie dough, and how big she can make each one.

Both happily learn these practical uses of arithmetic and geometry, and thereby develop their abilities to process logic, while each being involved in an activity they're particularly interested in.

We also find that showing them how to make things they enjoy and then sell is another inspiring way to learn basic math, writing, logistics, use of a computer, learning about banking, etc., while also learning basic skills of commerce. These things can be more fun with collaboration of others, whether in person or remotely, while helping to build relationships.

I'd add that we should recognize a large proportion of our learning occurs while simultaneously gaining relationship building skills—for example, in setting up and running an eBay store together, perhaps later even with other free homeschool friends.

You see, there is no limit in the different subjects they may become very interested in. From almost all such discoveries, they progress and continually grow knowledge and self-confidence.

Such is the true wealth of learning freely, that it can greatly empower our children in being able to create in life what they are most inspired to continue learning with.

As much as possible, we as parents must avoid free homeschooling being an unpleasant chore, which children will tend to avoid, or finish as soon as possible. We must inspire pleasure and great memories in learning so that our children will remain enthusiastic about continuing to gain knowledge and nurture relationships with confidence in themselves into adulthood and beyond.

7 Free Homeschool Curriculum

Great learning is possible through some of the following suggestions, but you will, together with your child, go on to develop a great many more besides.

If you don't yet have ideas, talk with your children and they'll come up with ideas that can align with what you're inspired by, and they can even unconsciously demonstrate what they like: Observe your children and they'll show their passions, naturally.

In this chapter, I won't go into the pitfalls and dangers that can present themselves, which homeschoolers and parents must be aware of—that's for another chapter: The Pro's and Cons of Homeschooling.

As we navigate life, through the challenges we and others face, I see time and time again the effects—both positive and negative—of **perceived reality** and what this can lead to in people's lives.

By perceived reality, I mean, **"how we see our lives and how we create the reality that supports the lives we believe we are living."**

To be an effective young adult in the future, it follows that a sound base for our thinking with which we can navigate the challenges ahead is strongly desirable, if not essential.

The sound base to which I refer is one which would contain the following, but there may be additional ones that you may want to add. This is a list for you to contemplate:

- Basic tidiness as a core attribute.

- Choice, and its impact in every aspect of their life.

- A realization that laziness, shyness and worry are some of the choices that do not serve us.

- The ability to communicate accurately and articulately.

- Deep thinking, contemplation and discussion.

- Development of cognitive logic.

- A core understanding that mistakes are an integral process of learning.

- Encouragement to imagine vividly.

- A natural passion for knowledge, developed through play and having fun.

- A well-balanced sense of humility, self-belief and confidence.

- Comfort with being around nature with the curiosity to learn from it.

- Compassion for others, instilled through life experiences and observations.

- A clear understanding of love, relationships and the power these give us.

- A deep value for integrity.

It's very beneficial to your son that he is allowed to take risks, provided they're not overly dangerous.

By giving children the responsibility of making important choices, they learn how to make good ones.[10]

We feel it's fine to let our kids climb trees, provided there are plenty of strong branches for them to hold on to. Conversely, we wouldn't allow them to climb a rock face without safety ropes, combined with explaining the importance of safety and discussing imagined examples.

In all activities, we must consider the dangers and make sure our kids are well protected, but not overly so. A few bruises and scrapes are part of character building.

THE BASICS

With our children, we have aimed to avoid encouraging bad habits. By rearing chicks, then later caring for chickens and goats, our children learn about taking responsibility for activities that are dependent on them, each and every day, for example.

• LAZINESS

This is a trait that doesn't serve any of us. It can lead to a huge amount of an individual's life less well spent if left to develop. Surely, it is better to concentrate on doing the things that are most enjoyed. I'm not suggesting it's not beneficial to lie in a field of summer flowers and watch the clouds float past above, sit by a stream and watch it flow by, watch the sun disappear on the horizon, or just contemplate quietly.[11]

• TIDINESS

This is a habit that can be passed on by example, as early as possible.

Researchers at Princeton University found in 2011 that untidiness is counterproductive for the focus on a particular task. They observed that the visual cortex can be overwhelmed by task-irrelevant objects, making it harder to concentrate and thereby complete a given task with efficiency.[12]

Try to instill tidiness by example, be prepared to do so calmly. We know this can be a tough ask at the most challenging of times, but persevere we must. The cost if we didn't instill such habits would likely otherwise be very high during their lives.

We got Akira a Lego mat, which becomes a tough bag when pulled shut via a string that runs along its circumference. I'd often tell him that everything has its place. Interestingly, it took a few years for him to appreciate the importance of tidiness through realizing he's lost hundreds of pieces of Lego by not taking precautions to avoid losing pieces.

Arina has lost books that form a series that she loved reading.

It's OK to learn from mistakes, but the aim of learning from them is to avoid making more of the same! Similarly, we've encouraged them to develop habits at a healthy level (not to excess) of cleanliness. They vacuum and tidy, sometimes do the dishes, sew and repair their clothes, clean windows, help clean the cars, tidy away camping gear, put their coats in the closet and not on the floor, etc.

Laziness and untidiness are poor habits I saw forming and worked on with our children as early as possible, but as gently as possible, especially with Akira. He finally learned the importance of not losing parts, or misplacing tools when working on his racing go-cart with me. Just one lost piece and it might not work properly ever again!

Arina learned the benefits of being tidy earlier, being more mature in her attention and listening at a younger age. Yes, girls certainly do appear to mature before boys.

• MANNERS

From an early age, be the best example of having manners, to instill in children how to behave around others. As parents, we avoid shouting or other forms of aggressive communication. We aim to instill calm, loving ways of communication in the way we speak with our children.

At the dinner table, we instill good table manners. As the children get older, we've encouraged them to make a habit of laying the table for family meals. A family dinner where all the family are together is an important time for bonding, and may be the only time in the day that the entire family is together. Make it count. Table manners, instilled throughout childhood, will stand your children in good stead for their adult lives. Well brought up adults will notice poor manners, which can reflect badly on those who don't know better.[13]

• GREAT COMMUNICATION SKILLS BEGIN AT HOME

Aim to have interesting and thought-provoking conversations at mealtimes and other family events. Encourage the children to describe events, activities and intentions in detail and with use of words they may not yet be familiar with. If they're emotional about something, ask them to share it. Talking like this, with regularity, helps build their self-confidence, so they become articulate in their speech.

• THE CORE IMPORTANCE OF A GOOD RELATIONSHIP BETWEEN COUPLES

Share openly about what is important to know for the adult life ahead of children. One aspect is what it is to be a healthy couple. If you consider yours a success story, or know someone who would be open about theirs, try to share the example: how the couple met, what dating was like, etc.

Many parents feel awkward about sharing their relationship with the children, but please consider the cost of not letting your children know. If your relationship is strong, why not share about what most parents hope their children will find someday? After all, the strongest relationship goal in the lives of most people is that between two life partners.

If our children have a good understanding, they too will know what they're looking for in future. We shared with each of our children the biological process through which they were conceived. Although to be frank, we wouldn't let them watch, they know we sometimes make love as husband and wife. They know that their sexual organs are private and to be respected by others, and vice versa.

Knowing is a form of protection from the many sexual perverts that can prey on children, given the opportunity. If an adult ever tries (God forbid) to touch ours inappropriately, they each know this isn't something they should tolerate, and to tell the person firmly to stop what they're doing immediately and let a responsible adult know, right away.

Sadly, sexual abuse happens a lot more than many of us realize. It's better our children know how to deal with inappropriate contact before it happens, from the earliest age possible.[14]

• SOCIALIZATION

As they've grown with each passing year, we've continued to facilitate and encourage our kids to socialize. If others aren't present, then write to them; grandparents, cousins, and friends love receiving letters or emails and most will respond. We encourage our kids to write essays about things they really enjoy or have a strong emotional feeling about, with pictures and photographs and publishing on a blog. It's always good to encourage them to speak or write about what they feel particularly strongly about.[15]

If a homeschoolers' group or association doesn't already exist where you live, create one! You can advertise to meet like-minded parents. Of course, in some countries you have to be careful of who you meet and befriend, but the genuine ones who you align with you'll strike up a friendship with quite quickly, and before too long you will find the group growing to have meetings in parks and other natural places where children enjoy themselves.

Being outdoors is a wonderfully involving way to learn about nature and life, while working with it and instilling natural wisdoms. If only schools put more importance on the understanding of nature, we'd all have a lot more respect for her and perhaps not find ourselves with a very damaged eco-system. A problem our children may have no choice but to face during their lifetimes.

One of the most rewarding ways is to find local retired people who may have extra time on their hands. If they're interested, invite them to interact with local homeschoolers. Retirees have a wealth of life experience they are often only too happy to share with young people.

For example, one of our community's homeschooler's grandparent wanted to make bird boxes to hang in their home's small forest. He found a free source of scrap wood and invited the children in our community to make the boxes.

Another parent knew an 84-year-old with a full woodwork hobby shop. The community has teamed up and are in the process of creating events for homeschooled children to learn how to use basic woodworking hand tools, and thereby create some beautiful bird boxes.

We have found other retirees who welcome children with whom they share their knowledge of how to grow vegetables, and their wonderful memories of the past. Another two retirees with an interest in racing go-carts have helped Akira and me.

The children learn so much from these wiser and more experienced elders, but also discover the great worth of relationships developed with them. In return, they get to relive what it's like to discover exciting things for the first time through seeing the excitement in children's eyes, and in this way, laughter, energy, and bonds are increasingly created in our local communities.

• SELF-DEVELOPMENT COURSES

This is a category not to be missed. There is only a paragraph when I could passionately write a chapter or an entire book on the subject. I would strongly recommend parents investigate this work first, then through the many positive changes within themselves and relationships between one another, be an example to your children and encourage them to study. I have learned through Landmark Worldwide,[16] as have Yuko and the kids (three-day course also available for young people), but there are other amazing courses from the likes of Tony Robbins who has coached some of the world's top athletes, politicians, musicians, and most successful CEOs.

What can be learned opens the door to a whole realm of possibilities. Not least, such courses greatly enhance the ability to create valuable lifelong relationships.

Don't pass up the opportunity for your family to live much better and more powerful lives!

• LANGUAGES

Yours may be a marriage of a mix of cultures and languages. If so, then you have additional learning possibilities from the day each of your children are born. Speak with them in as many different languages as possible, with regularity. As small children, their brains are like sponges, eager to absorb volume.

Yuko is Japanese and speaks English, I have learned to speak five languages during my life. We first taught our children spoken English and Japanese, also reading to them at night. By the age of four, each could converse in both languages and we have seen other multilingual children speak three or four languages. There's no limit to what they are capable of. Make them believe in their abilities, not be held back by what they believe they aren't capable of.

Initially, through phonics we taught each of them to know the sound of letters (with particular regard to English language) and how letters are strung together, to write words. Using this skill, we slowly progressed through books, each at their own pace.

• MATHEMATICS

Our children are both good at math and enjoy it. That's half the battle, but of course there are some days when they're not very inspired. A reputable workbook series is good. Take time to research what may be good for your children. From around 10 years of age, consider getting them a Rubiks® Cube, which helps teach logic, which goes hand-in-hand with math. Consider that basic mathematical understanding is also enhanced through learning a musical instrument, but not solely by such.

• SELF-DISCIPLINE TO STUDY

As ours had each covered the first couple of years of elementary school, they'd already gotten into the routine of workbooks and worksheets for math and Japanese characters too. By spending time with them (doesn't have to be for very long each day, 20-30 minutes per subject is ample), they can gain confidence, and hopefully find enjoyment in the methods of learning we introduce.

After some time, they have both become used to studying by themselves and asking for help if they get stuck. Once they found books in the library they enjoyed, the flow continued without need for much encouragement, if any.

The above are what we consider to be the primary basics of homeschool learning.

Make all activities safe and fun, so the children enjoy—and your work will be lessened considerably in future.

OTHER GREAT BENEFICIAL ACTIVITIES

The following are examples of other activities our children have participated in as a part of their learning, whether outdoor, underwater, or at home, as a means to plant seeds of possibilities for your children.

• PLAY IN NATURE

Grow foods from seed, read about and plant small fruit trees in the garden, to then see them grow. We eventually harvest and eat the produce, juice it, or make jams and marmalade. It is possible to grow foods from an apartment's city balcony, but desirable to have larger spaces if possible.

• NATURAL COMMUNITY

Find a friendly neighbor, organic farmer or permaculturalist and ask to do some interesting activities together. Better to find someone who grows things naturally, as you'll see how nature works.

We recently harvested part of a crop of sweet potato, as a group of homeschoolers. The children always enjoy these activities, while familiarizing themselves with life in the earth, such as small beetles, worms, small lizards, etc. (Parents who were brought up being afraid of critters must avoid passing on such fears; I concealed my irrational fears and have chosen to confront them, picking up praying mantis when Akira was afraid of them. He picks up anything now.)

• ENCOURAGE STUDY OF PERMACULTURE SYSTEMS[17]

Research, design and make a small chicken coop, possibly using old pallets as (free) material. Learn about how chicks develop while caring for small chicks obtained from a farmer. Ask for as much advice as possible, what they eat, how many boys (one or two— if you can bear the crowing of a full -grown rooster later!) per 12 chicks. Watch them grow up, while being cared for by the children. Later, full grown females will lay eggs, which adds to the fun in keeping chickens.

Once kids know how to raise small chicks, if you have a friendly farmer (or permaculturalist!), we'd encourage you to obtain an inexpensive incubator and try hatching eggs. Children's eyes light up when they see a chick pecking through its shell and pop out. Reading and watching videos will keep kids learning useful biology for hours and inspires continual curiosity and development of activities around science.

Make a worm farm from plastic boxes and organic waste. Kids can use these worms to help encourage healthy soil in their gardening projects and begin to learn that everything has connections in nature and there is no waste!

• CRAFTS AND HOBBIES

There are many possibilities, but a few examples: drawing, painting, jewelry making, pottery, sculpture, woodworking, model making, shaping wood, leathercraft, and many more.
    • Research and make a small tool shed together, using basic materials, or even dismantle and improve someone's old donated shed. Hang tools on walls and on a sturdy rail, using self-shaped and blunt-ended s-hooks. Learn how to keep tools tidy, free of corrosion and well accounted for, so they're always there when in need.

• PUBLIC SPEAKING[18]

Sign up for speech competitions, even if your child is shy, provided you're not forcing her, but she will go on her own accord. Public speaking during childhood is a great way to get over the fear of speaking before crowds or performing in front of them.

For Arina, participating in the Kokorozashi Speech Presentation, a finalist over two consecutive years, was a major milestone as part of her homeschooling. Her confidence and resolve grew tremendously, and I would strongly recommend participation in similar events, even online if that is all that becomes available for a time.

• PRESENTATION SKILLS

Enter contests for talents, which can include anything from art to robotic programing. Contests are a great way to also explore public speaking and the progress it offers in creating relationships with others that we don't realize are possible at first. Encourage your child to present and speak about their favorite activity or hobby. It's the subject they most often share with us, and which they feel the most naturally compelled to talk about. Free homeschoolers can learn a **lot** with hobbies. You'll be amazed!

• PRACTICAL SKILLS

Whenever a parent does DIY work around the home, try to include the children if appropriate. They may learn yet another useful skill.

• TECHNICAL SKILLS

For more technical and IT-minded children, encourage them to learn how to design and 3-D print plastics, then create products they can sell. It is also possible to create simple mechanical replacement/upgrade parts for hobbies from inexpensive components, easily found and available online (I'll soon be showing Akira how to make a product from $10-15 worth of simple mechanical parts, to sell at $50, for example).

• COMMERCIAL SKILLS

Take any sellable thing that is not too fragile or easily perishable etc. and sell it at a local market. This is a great way to strike up new friendships, as other children will see items or activities they're interested in. It is possible to do this as a group of homeschoolers, offering wares they have a particular passion for creating or farming—and also a useful way to earn some pocket money.

• EXPEDITIONS

Organize outdoor events, from hiking trips (usually for older children, but younger children can be accompanied by a parent), through to overnight trips on small mountains during appropriate seasons when safe to do so.

Do group cycling expeditions, with a particular challenging goal in mind. By setting children a tough but achievable task, we help them build determination, self-belief, and bravery.

During outdoor events such as these, where permitted and safe to do so under adult supervision, have small bonfires at night, where young kids can socialize after a day's expedition, to share and cement experiences and friendships. Memories made during evenings such as these are not usually easily forgotten.

• SWIMMING—EXCELLENT EXERCISE

All children love water, provided they don't have any early traumatic experiences. Keep them safe, but while observing and being ready to help, let them take small risks provided there's no danger. A child who learns to swim well at a young age is endowed with a great many more abilities to enjoy a richer life than a child who is made to feel afraid of water. Within one to two years, our children have both become excellent swimmers.

At any opportunity you are presented with, take children swimming in natural environments. Our children each learned basics of swimming by wearing a wetsuit with built-in floatation when jumping off a pontoon into deep water and watching how Mama and Papa swim in the summer.

• EXPLORE NATURE UNDERWATER

Children love to go snorkeling in clear water and thereby soon learn to hold their breath and stay underwater and improve their technique. They can also learn much by observation. Later, if you've some spare money, take them scuba diving. The world's coral is fast being destroyed by rising sea temperatures and excessive nutrients being washed into the sea. Give them every possibility to enjoy what may disappear in future if man doesn't find sustainable solutions to enhance the growth of nature, as opposed to destroying it.

• INDIVIDUAL INTERESTS

Seek out lessons in particular subjects. Akira is clearly interested in technical things and likes to make contraptions that move, so we are looking for someone who can teach him programing skills, so he can learn how to code and design simple solutions. In doing this, he would learn how to 3-D scan, design and print, and thereby be able to start making his own components for things he invents during play in future.

For children with a curiosity for engineering, as Akira has in abundance, we would recommend encouraging its growth. We have bought and sailed small R/C cars, boats, drones, then graduated on to R/C planes. He has taken some apart, to create (and sometimes fail to create) his own designs.

Budding engineers take things apart. It's just a part of their learning. Let them, but encourage progress and completion where possible.

• PLAY WITH EDUCATIONAL TOYS

Lego has been great for Akira, helping him develop creativity when making things of his own design. Monopoly has been a good game to help introduce the art of business, negotiation and even collaboration, while using basic arithmetic and reading skills.

We intend to offer a regularly updated choice of educational toys as part of the online chapter of this book (visit www.howtohomeschool.life

• TAKE PRIVATE CLASSES—ENCOURAGE DEVELOPMENT OF INDIVIDUAL PASSIONS

Take coaching classes in the activities each child is most interested in. Arina began with piano classes, then progressed to jazz piano, then on to singing, for which she discovered a greater passion. She's also studied ballet since she was four, and so has learned to be elegant when dancing.

Our son has been learning martial arts since the age of five. He didn't enjoy karate but wanted to move to aikido, which he has enjoyed a lot more since. We can see he is interested in guitar and drums, as well as hip-hop dance, so we remain on the lookout for lessons in these, always aiming to leave the door open. Sometimes, it's too early to try a new interest. If the seed doesn't bloom, it doesn't mean it's dead. We can gently continue providing the nutrition for its growth, without attachment to the desired result.

• PASSIONS FOR ACTIVITIES SHARED BETWEEN A CHILD AND PARENT

Where a parent shares the same enthusiasm as his/her child, this should be encouraged. In my case, it's motorsports, and currently go-cart racing with Akira. A lot of engineering and the understanding of simple principles of physics can be learned through this hobby. Valuable bonding and creation of wonderful memories can develop between a child and his parent when a shared passion is developed and enjoyed together, which can even turn into a shared interest that continues to be enjoyed through adulthood.

• PASSIONS FOR ACTIVITIES SHARED BETWEEN FRIENDS

When the opportunity arises, where a group of homeschooled children gel well together, encourage further bonding. For example, if they enjoy playing with instruments, suggest they form a band and play simple things together. If a passion for creating music develops, take it from there.

• MARTIAL ARTS

Discuss with your child and explore possible martial arts activities they may find interesting. Martial arts are a great way to develop self-discipline, attention to detail, self-respect and respect for others, fitness, and of course, the ability to defend oneself. Judo is one of the most basic martial arts and is a sport that is enjoyed and children can develop, all the way to Olympic level. There are many: karate, Thai boxing, aikido, ju-jitsu, capoeira and many more.

• SAILING IS MAGICAL FOR CHILDREN

If the opportunity presents itself, give your children the opportunity to learn how to sail a small dinghy (under supervision and with qualified instruction). There's magic in exploring a lake, all without the use of a motor, and children learn basic physics, even understanding how a bird can fly, much as a boat can sail upwind. If you have a station wagon and a safe place to sail, it's possible to buy an old windsurf board and sails for very low cost and enable children to learn to sail that way too. It's also a great way to keep them fit.

• ADVENTURES IN TRAVELING

Travel and explore different places, as wide and as different as possible. This is a great way to learn about local history and how things have developed. Also, as we have seen here in Japan, children can learn of the skills that are dying away with passing generations, and perhaps even take an interest in studying a few. There are a great many skills that are disappearing, nowadays—such as traditional Japanese joinery for earthquake-proof building, for example.

• UNDERSTAND GOVERNMENT

Arrange to meet with a local politician such as the mayor and ask him to explain what his daily duties are. Learn about how local government works and ask the official to describe how they got into a career like this and why. It's best to come prepared with a list of questions that homeschoolers may want to ask. In this way, children may begin to gain an understanding of and interest in how local government works.

• UNDERSTANDING HOW BUSINESS WORKS

Arrange visits to local businesses, perhaps as a homeschooler's expedition. Learn how products are manufactured, packaged, shipped or marketed. Meet the company director and ask that he shares the story of his struggles to build the company into what it has become, so children gain some understanding of what it takes to start a new venture. Arrange visits to banks, farm cooperatives, and as many businesses as possible.

Find out how technology is changing their businesses and what challenges they see looming with the advent of AI. The more that children understand of the world of adults, the sooner they may begin to see a niche they are inspired by or discover others they hadn't known before. When companies hear of how unique homeschooled children can be and witness the bright inquisitiveness that can exist in their eyes, they too are often inspired by the children they see.

• JUST PLAY!

Last, but one of the most important—encourage your child to play with other children, regardless of age. Ours play very well with younger children who visit our home with their parents. Equally, they both have older friends with whom they like to socialize. Their more developed social skills help make their conversational abilities all the more interesting, but to be able to play like a child is a great skill set that many of us forget as we grow up. Those of our children who can always remember will offer a great advantage for their own families someday.

8 Facing Your Homeschool Fears

"I never teach my pupils. I only attempt to provide conditions in which they can learn."

- ALBERT EINSTEIN

"True homeschoolers understand that learning is an adventure to be experienced and cherished, not a chore to muddle through to get a grade."

- J. ALLEN WESTON
Executive director www.nationalhomeschoolassociation.com

The idea of developing your child's ideal style of free homeschooling can seem daunting if not impossible at first. We've been here ourselves when we first began, and empathize with what you may be facing.

In these early circumstances, it can be useful to ask yourself what it is you don't want. It may be that you don't feel it's beneficial to invoke rigorous schedules, or to teach by boring repetitive memorization. Maybe you don't feel inspired at the idea of shouting at your children or intimidating them into doing things they would not otherwise.

Unlike schools, where the notion is that one-size-fits-all, at home we have the valuable luxury of making it fit our children's ways of learning, so their passions are ignited. It's often not easy. If only I had a crystal ball to show you, the answer really is right before your eyes.

When homeschooling doesn't work, your child will tell you. His tears and frustrations will be real. The sparkle in his eyes is also real and so is the zone you'll naturally both want to focus on.

We often forget that we don't have to teach our kids math in the same way we learned at school. I can teach my son through practical ways. I don't need to succumb to the temptation to buy that boxed set of math books, in the possibly unrealistic hope he'll become engrossed in them. I can discuss the content and encourage him. Maybe even interact and make it more fun, using beans or coins.

Play a game of backgammon, which can be a wonderfully fun way to build mental arithmetic skills in calculating fast!

We don't have to get our kids up at the crack of dawn, unless there's an inspiring reason for this to be necessary, such as caring for livestock or doing something extra special. They can and do learn a lot faster at home than at school, so why train them to live in the grown-up world of being up and ready to start their factory shift at 8:00 am or earlier?

Ask yourself if the thoughts of compliance with the ways that others learn now and the temptation to emulate them are of your own insecurities about taking responsibility for your child's education. Do we need to stick to the ways of others just to be more acceptable to the world as it is now when the world outside is morphing into a wallowing sea of fear right before our eyes, and if unchecked, will look vastly different by the time our children become adults?

We are in the midst of the Fourth Industrial Revolution, where industry, commerce, and the wealthiest world leaders align in the vision that AI will take many of the jobs that exist today.[19] If their vision is allowed to become our reality, bank branches will be largely unmanned. Jobs to perform mundane tasks at stores, say as a sales clerk, will disappear. So too will jobs to drive, then later even pilot vehicles, warehouse logistics will become increasingly automated, and so on…

Businesses will become much more online and as technology advances, the talents that will be most sought after will be those that align with technology yet to be developed. Or will it?

What humanity believes is largely what humanity lives into. We, the people, have the power as the majority to create the better future we are inspired to live into.

The world will need gifted technological innovators, people who understand and can work with nature, individuals who can help those who are unable to figure out how to reinvent their careers, teachers who understand the power of learning through passion and the burning desire to help others, great engineers able to design and build the infrastructural changes that will make the most of living with nature, and not against it.

Doctors with genuine ethics and compassion will be called for, who can offer us the natural medicines of healing that the industrial complex pharmaceutical industry has replaced with synthesized chemicals that suppress disease but don't cure. We need great thinkers who are able to work with humanity and not against it, to build a better tomorrow.

Although some of the most special individuals may rise from the ashes of what remains of the current school education system, as it becomes ever less social, while morphing into less costly and more controlling online schooling, we believe there is brighter hope, happiness, and fulfillment through facilitating the greatest childhoods for our children.

A childhood which offers freedom to be, natural wisdom, time to contemplate, experimentation, learning positively from the process of making and correcting mistakes, an upbringing with love, strength in relationship building and strong self-belief, and a world where we are an inclusive society built on decency, honesty, compassion for all, and a willingness to share generously.

Can you see the power your child can absorb if we endow her with attributes such as the above when we look at the alternative that may prevail if we just sit back and let state schools be responsible for our children's learning and development?

The unknown world of the future can be a scary one if we perceive it as such, but we have the power to manifest a better one with our children.

"What we are seeking is seeking us."

– LILWEN SELINA JOYNSON

We can rise to the challenges we encounter by staying flexible enough to change, to adapt, to experiment, be playful and to try something new. The more willing we are to evolve and adapt, the more options we create and thereby opportunities, which will continually reveal themselves for even more creativity.

We can bring our own style, love and personalities to the kitchen or dining table where our kids spend time learning. Compared to the classroom, they're much more inspired by our love and commitment to them than to the schoolteacher dividing her time between 35 children and a set limit of time per class. We homeschoolers can spend an hour, two, a morning or even an entire day studying what is making their eyes light up.

YOUR CHILD'S INTERESTS LEAD TO THE MOST EFFECTIVE CURRICULUM.

George Bernard Shaw has many excellent quotes and is an author whose writing I would encourage anybody to explore.

Here are a few poignant quotes from him:

"The only time my education was interrupted was when I was in school."

"Progress is impossible without change; and those who cannot change their minds cannot change anything."

"Life isn't about finding yourself. Life is about creating yourself."

Natural learning is facilitated by providing the spaces and resources in which and from which our children can learn.

This morning, Yuko told me she and the kids were off to see another natural farmer, to talk about the environment. They sent me beautiful pictures of the scenery around, and although I'm not there as I sit here writing, I know they're having a lot of fun. They're sitting talking, sharing and wondering about what they're discussing, while absorbing the sounds of nature and being present in the environment of today.

Later, they'll meet with more people, mostly adults, who will be especially interested in our daughter's thoughts and words about the environment. Our son, keen to get his share of attention, will no doubt be entertaining people with his wit and charm and thereby also gaining from being immersed among other people he doesn't yet know. They'll learn new things about natural plant growth in many ways without even realizing they're learning new things.

If they weren't excited and inspired through being in nature, then equally their mother may take them to visit a factory making something they're interested in, or any range of activities where they might learn. Someday under suitably safe supervision, for example, I'd like for them to be able to visit a fishing environment and learn what the old fishermen might share, or even go out on a fishing boat on an early morning to see and experience how the fish are caught.

Another day, I'd like them to visit a machine shop and see how pieces of metal are shaped and welded, or perhaps even take a tour of a car factory.

Another day, perhaps they could visit a computer games development company, or even a design studio to see how a creative office or corporate environment can be.

I'd like them to see how a fridge or air conditioning system works, which is just one of infinite examples of physics and chemistry in practical use, which we can then discuss later when asking, "How does the expansion of gases work to cool an environment?" (possibly while spraying a volatile substance such as alcohol under pressure on to their hand, to illustrate).

Even around our home, they sometimes get the opportunity to see a new house being built. It's educational to observe and understand how things work!

The possibilities for what they may see and learn are endless and a means through which they can get a broad range of experiences, seeing how things work, or how they're made. Their potential for possibilities that may become useful in their own adult lives someday will continue to grow.

Activities such as these offer a richer flavor of education that leaves children with more questions than in a conventional classroom environment, where they may be found looking out the window in boredom, or wonder at just how the world around them works.

What we have always found to work well is gently introducing children to new things that they may be inspired by, and more often than not, they will take up the challenge to become interested and absorbed, losing track of time and enjoying what they are discovering. It's wonderful to see their growth and not least the relationships they continue to build along the way.

Quite naturally they'll zero in on new kids of similar age whenever at someplace new, and especially when given the opportunity, they'll happily spend time with adults, provided they are involved with and paying attention to whatever activity the kids, too, are inspired by.

And so, relationship building continues to develop and day by day, doors they didn't yet realize existed continue to open for more discoveries.

I'd like to share two stories which illustrate what becomes possible through inspired interests, as two touching examples.

I had a dear friend and talented teacher of permaculture, who works with children and adults alike, visit our home only yesterday afternoon. We spent a fascinating four hours discussing many different topics. Both being dedicated parents, we discussed their progress.

He had wanted to see our homeschooled kids, knowing they'd be home. By the time he left in the late afternoon, he had clearly been inspired by their progress—even Akira's who had only been homeschooling for a couple of months at that time.

He commented on the excellence of their English accents. He'd been in awe of Arina's art and both their abilities to be self-motivated. He especially liked seeing their enthusiasm and freedom of being, where our eight-year-old son was keen to interact with him and felt totally comfortable being around an adult he didn't remember meeting before (he had, but like most children of his age had forgotten memories playing at a beach five years earlier).

Phillip shared a story of how he and his team had created a permaculture garden in a school in Tokyo and how some of the teachers, children, and mothers had become involved in it. This was a story spanning a couple of years, which I'd known about through our conversations.

There were many children who were inspired, but two individuals particularly shone and they were children who hadn't fitted well into the school's society. One was a girl, starting the project aged 10, who was very shy and would avoid contact with anybody. The other was a similarly aged young boy. Very thin and awkward. Not prone to much interaction with others at all.

When chicks were introduced, the girl became very involved with them. Her enthusiasm was insatiable and every day she'd be with the chicks, making sure they were well looked after, while studying everything she could about chickens. Within a couple of months, everybody knew she was the one to ask when knowledge about chickens was sought. She understood their roles in a permaculture food system as far as preparation of the ground for planting, their manure as fertilizer, etc.

The boy had found his niche in this project too and was now seen to be gaining confidence in leaps and bounds. Where before he would have made himself almost invisible when around others, now, when my friend asked for a volunteer to help with part of a building project, his hand shot up with the urgency of someone who was determined to be part of completion of the tasks at hand.

They had to bring down trees, which they used for making the large garden's outdoor furniture. Week by week, with my friend's visits to the school, the children's teachers, the kids, and the headmaster had collaborated to create something special.

Food was now being grown there and mothers would spend time planting and chatting. It became a place where more and more people would congregate and, of course, children would play. The wooden garden furniture was painted bright colors and as the chickens grew, a coop was erected.

The project gained recognition and two of the children were selected to present the story to two important Japanese government officials. The two children that the school had selected were the girl and boy above. It was a proud day for the school, but most importantly for these two individuals.

Tokyo, being a place where space is at a premium, meant that this beautiful and flourishing permaculture area of a public school began to attract attention, and although most of it was positive, there was a less desirable type from the neighbors, working in an office building which faced on to the project.

Apparently, the head teacher hadn't gone through the proper

channels to gain permission for the project, and so phone calls from typically polite, irate but determined neighbors to the local government's education minister eventually led to the decision that the permaculture garden had to go. The headmaster was instructed to relay the bad news to the children.

The young girl, who'd previously been completely withdrawn and was now proud to be referred to as "Chicken Mama," was at first devastated at the news, but behind those eyes was now a determined resolve.

She rounded up all the pupils who had been involved with the project and together they arranged a large meeting with the headmaster, where they explained the importance of the project and that they were not prepared to give it up now, for it to be destroyed after all the work they'd put in and all the learning they'd gotten out of it.

This project had to stay, for the sake of future students who'd be involved with it.

The headmaster was so touched by this event that he relayed it to the local education office, who in turn conceded that the project should remain, even though it hadn't been created through the proper channels or funding.

Although this is a story about a wonderful development in the grounds of a school, it's notable that the learning and development for children wasn't through the conventional methods we associate with classroom learning.

A young girl and boy who weren't integrating well with the rest of the school had found their mojo and in turn gained the respect and acceptance of fellow classmates through what had just started out as seeds of possibility!

Phillip shared that the children had since moved on from primary school to Junior High. Despite the disruptions of Covid-19, they were still involved in the project, sharing their knowledge with other children.

He himself had since stopped teaching the program, but parents, teachers, and new students had taken the reins and it remained alive and well, albeit different. Such projects are started by visionaries like Phillip and are then left to continue to develop through other people who are inspired by the seeds of possibility sown. Such seeds can be sown anywhere they're likely to flourish and we never know what other unexpectedly beautiful results may blossom.

Our afternoon yesterday also included another inspiring story he shared which, in turn, I'd like to share with you. It's not something I want to share so much as a suggestion, but more as an insight of how animals can be so powerful for a child's learning.

Yorita San was someone who'd had trouble as a child. He'd not fitted well within the school system and had never really understood what his purpose in life was while studying at school. At times he had even been suicidal.

Sadly, today, in the environment of the militaristic system of schooling in Japan and moreover in the dystopian world some of our children are living in, where some kids are feeling a sense of hopelessness and experience depression, there are many children who consider, attempt, or at worst succeed in suicide.

Yorita San is a man who learned deep compassion as a result of the suffering he went through as a child. He has dedicated his life to making a difference.

He started his first alternative school in Okinawa, the sub-tropical islands of Japan. His vision, turned to reality, is a primary school for children who find themselves unable to integrate with others. A free school (as in "freedom to learn") with a focus on living in the **present**.

The beautiful idea is that the teachers at Yorita San's school are horses. Yes, you read that right: Horses. "Horses?" you might ask, as I did. At first, I thought by "horse" he was speaking in a symbolic term, but then I began to understand what Phillip was describing.

Yes, horses.

See, a horse is an animal that doesn't dwell on the past, nor does he look to the future. He is inspired by the realm of now, and to get a horse to do what you'd like, even if it's to move from one side to another so a student can clean his stable, the student too must relate his communication with the horse to doing something now too.

Throughout the day, the students make relationships with the horses that are noble, beautiful animals. I have since met Lilwen Selina Joynson (author of *Making a Difference*), a lady who works with horses (Eagala), with animal-assisted therapy to help heal those who are suffering from depression and related difficulties. She was particularly excited to hear of Yorita San's primary school projects.

I've recalled the two stories above as I feel a lot of would-be free homeschooling parents are now searching, some even in desperation, to find a better solution for their children, some of whom may be terribly affected by what is happening to their lives since the Coronavirus era began. We feel a deep empathy for those who are suffering, and this is the main reason I have written this book during these times, and why we are committed to continuing in this line of work. Yuko and I are committed to helping as many children as we can.

There are many theories today, most of which I find ever less interest in researching. To look at the doom and gloom doesn't inspire. It may make us weaker in our resolve.

We find it more powerful to look at what has actually happened and continues to develop and, where we can, stand up to help others.

In these strange times, we see the global scale erosion of relationships. We see the need to rebuild, create, and inspire people to build relationships with one another, as not just a means of reversal, but toward building a better future than we were each previously living in. The more of us who join together in homeschooling from a place in the heart, the stronger we, as a tribe, become.

I firmly believe it is in strong relationships with others that we find the greatest wealth of life. It is the wealth we will each hold dearest in our last hour, more valuable than health. The relationships with loved ones by our side will reduce the pain we might be suffering. It will be the strength of those relationships which will be worth the most to each of us, not money accumulated, regardless of how large or small, in those last moments.

Our heroes are most often the ones that make us shed the most worthwhile tears, where with each tear our eyes shed, we acknowledge them. We can each be heroes for our children and others. We each have the power within us to choose how we direct ourselves.

Those who fully appreciate the contents of the complete paragraph directly above and live it will have access to a power that humanity seldom discover for themselves.

So, encourage your children to grow a love for building great relationships with others. They will be richer with a wealth of happiness in life that money alone could never buy for them. Contemplate and take your time understanding the infinite wisdom and power of relationships can inspire others through the love for humanity they see in your children's eyes.

Lastly, this being a chapter about facing your fears, while thinking of what many are facing now in their day-to-day lives during the Covid-19 era, I would like to leave you with my thoughts on fear, and love:

Fear is debilitating. It denies us powerful resolve, and we shrink back, willing to do or not, as may be required of us, so we don't have to face what we are afraid of.

Fear confiscates our dreams and as we are wrapped in it, we dare not, because what if…?

Life as we knew it has been a series of terrible disasters, most of which never actually took place. We shouldn't be controlled by fear, but instead be in control of 'it'!

Laugh in the face of fear and know that we are here for only the briefest flicker of a flame.

We must burn in this brief flicker in the brightest light possible, to manifest our greatest dreams, to share and be an inspiration for others to do the same, or more.

We can join hands and share love, knowing the more we create, the more abundant love becomes.

A genuine smile, an act of selfless kindness, to touch somebody's heart, makes our own heart resonate with happiness, so spread love and help heal humanity.

When we, as humanity, join to care for one another and refuse to live in the false and heartless world that is being created to imprison our hearts, fear will be something we can look back at and laugh at how unscary it really was all along. We're already free, some of us just haven't realized it yet.

9 Free Homeschool Resources

The main concern niggling at the back of our minds as we studied and compiled the list of resources below is about how computers, whilst useful and essential for most, are tools that if overused, can lead to an unhealthy dependency. We, as parents, must ensure we don't let the habit of staring at screens affect our children's lives too much.

How much is too much? That's for each parent to decide. About five or six hours a week is too much for some, and too little for others, but we'd urge you to watch your child's reactions as you ask him to switch off the computer. Once started, it can be difficult to reverse the fascination.

With ourselves, our kids tend to gravitate toward spending time outdoors, making things, and being involved in activities that involve more physical actions. We've seen kids grown into adulthood who had their lives very detrimentally affected through video games, social media, and other screen addictions, so getting too acquainted with such things would concern me and Yuko.

But we realize not all parents feel the same way. Some may even encourage learning through games and unschooling online courses. It should also be the child's choice, and provided it's not dangerous, that is something we would respect, but be unlikely to recommend.

Please do be mindful that children are happier when they're using their bodies to do things, rather than sitting in front of a screen.

And so, with the above caveat in mind, we have spent much time searching, to compile the list below.

Searching "Free Schooling" or "Free Homeschool Resources," most of the results appear to point at substitutes for conventional schooling.

It's likely this would be just what most parents look for, especially in these times of Coronavirus, where children are stuck at home, unable to attend school as normal, and parents are desperate to find a solution.

Few parents initially searching will see the incredible benefits of what can become possible for our children, even if at first sampled alongside conventional schooling, especially during this ongoing Coronavirus crisis.

Searching the keywords, "Unschooling Resources" reveals more inspiring results, but we'd hazard a guess this is not necessarily what most parents would gravitate toward, with the phrase beginning with "Unschooling." Some of us may find the word "Unschooling" unfortunate, since it also implies undoing learning, which is not what it does.

Perhaps there's another aspect. Is it not us, the parents, who may benefit from un-learning how we were educated?

Free Schooling is perhaps a more eloquent way to describe it, but in the context of learning naturally at home, we may prefer to describe what we do as "Free Homeschooling."

The following is a resource guide compiled by ourselves, which offers useful websites and information which we hope may lead to further exploration and discoveries:

https://www.thehomeschoolmom.com/waiting-for-unschooling-to-work/
• Shay Seabourne tells of her triumphs and tribulations with unschooling, in a very resonant way.
This site offers an incredible scope and array of topics. Well worth taking the time to explore.

https://unschoolers.org/why-unschool/
• A short, truthful and compelling introduction to what real free homeschooling is all about.

https://unschoolingmom2mom.com/unschooling-resources/
• A good source for initial information. Also has a useful video which can be shared with others who would like an introduction to what free schooling can be.

www.suepatterson.com
• Author of *Homeschooled Teens*, a collection of accounts of unschooling from 75 different teenagers.

https://happinessishereblog.com/
• A great free homeschooler's blog by a family who share their beautiful progress.

https://livingjoyfully.ca/podcast-2/
• Pam Laricchia is an author and long-time unschooling mom from Ontario, Canada. Hosts the weekly Exploring Unschooling podcast.

https://www.johnholtgws.com/writing-about-john-holt
• John Holt was a pioneer whose ideas planted the seed that has developed into Free Schooling.

https://iaswece.org/waldorf-education/what-is-waldorf-education/
• A source of information to explain the ethos behind an early Waldorf education. Although usually found in a Steiner-styled kindergarten (such as Asoubimura), this natural learning can be enjoyed in a homeschool environment.

https://simplycharlottemason.com/what-is-the-charlotte-mason-method/
• Using literature within "living books." Children are encouraged to describe their understanding instead of doing tests.

https://nationalhomeschoolassociation.com
• National H.Q. for homeschooling in America. Providing support, programs, activities, and resources to homeschoolers.

https://talkbox.mom/ball/
• A free introduction to learning a foreign language, an easy and painless way for children with particular interest in languages to enjoy while learning.

https://www.khanacademy.org/
• The main website for Khan Academy. A non-profit studying resource for most conventional subjects. It does include some academic learning-based tutorials, as well as resources that some children may be particularly attracted by, as topics they have a passion for.

https://learn.khanacademy.org/khan-academy-kids/
• Free, fun educational programs for children aged two to eight.

https://funancialfreedom.com/
• The aim of FUNancial Freedom is simple. To teach seven- to 17-year-olds to become financially smart.

Teaches through interactive video courses, and what child doesn't want to know how to make money?

The sooner they learn, the better they may become at being financially free as children!

https://code.org/learn
• If your kids enjoy Minecraft, this is a useful way to learn, without having to find local classes or travel. We would advise caution with letting kids spend too much time in front of a screen.

https://simplycoding.org/
• More advanced online classes, with a 10-day free trial. Perhaps a better learning experience once your child's interest has been piqued.

https://teachkidsengineering.com/
• A resource for children interested in learning. We would strongly encourage a hands-on approach primarily, just tinkering with fun things, before moving on to learning online. For example, invite kids to play with a Rubik's Cube and try to figure it out before watching how to solve it!

https://store.bravewriter.com/
• A way to learn literature through living books, with inspired discussion. We're big advocates of inspired reading. Well worth exploring.

https://outschool.com/
• Over 100,000 different classes, available online for most subjects. A place where children can choose what they want to learn, with infinite choice. From guitar lessons to cooking. It's all there!

https://www.prodigygame.com/main-en/

• Games are something we'd advise caution with if exploring, since one may inspire curiosity about more, and the dangers that lie within, but this website offers fun ways to explore basic math.

https://www.thoughtco.com/free-homeschool-resources-4151635

• I wasn't sure if I should include this link but thought it may be useful for parents who may be experiencing financial challenges. Know that your determination to provide the best you can in the face of adversity can be very inspiring to your kids. Here you will find a resource all about homeschooling for free.

None of the above are my own personal recommendations (we have developed our own far more direct and natural resources for learning, which are shared as the contents of this book). These are the resources which many other free homeschoolers have found useful. It is up to you and your child to decide which most resonate, then explore and see.

An endless choice of other unschooling resources can be found by searching online. Our aim is not to list every possible one that children may find fascinating. That would be an infinite challenge! These should get you started, while watching what your children are most "lit-up" by.

Remember also, there are many other ways to learn, sometimes much closer to your home than you may think. Look out for those who have a passion for what they're sharing, it can be infectious!

Piano and guitar scholars and all sorts of musicians yearn to share their passion with young people who are on their frequency. Create ways with your children to meet such people and enjoy engaging in such challenges together.

There are many woodwork hobbyists who would love the opportunity to disseminate their knowledge. Find one who understands how children play, while being mindful they don't necessarily know the dangers of using sharp tools and are willing to show children how to do things right.

Many great gardeners, cooks, dancers, and people from all walks of life are out there, many of whom are happy, retired people, often with time on their hands. Many of these people have genuine warm hearts and would be only too happy to share time with you and your children. Some will benefit from payment; some will love a warm home-cooked meal and companionship. Some will just be happy to give, without expectation of anything in return. Make friends, share life and build community. In this way, you can gain much more life experience than through online courses.

We hope with some of the resources we have listed you can gain full conviction in your choices, together with your child, and choose not to be concerned by what others may think, but what activity may benefit your child's brightest possible future. Never forget—it's through play that young children learn the most naturally and self-beneficially.

MEETING THE CHALLENGES

10 Health is Our Wealth

The majority of us take our health for granted, and especially when young, are steadfastly unaware of what may be early signs of poor health choices, which if left unchecked will detrimentally affect our future health.

"Let thy food be thy medicine and medicine be thy food."

- HIPPOCRATES (400 BC)

Few youngsters contemplate that without health, we would be unable to partake in many activities that keep life enjoyable to the fullest. Many young families allow their children to consume foods and drinks containing very unhealthy ingredients, such as Aspartame, Imidacloprid, and many GMO-based foods, to name just a few, of which many people are unaware.

For each family there will be many, and this chapter is not intended to single out what are the right and wrong choices. What may not work for us may not be the same for you your family. There are countless books to read on health and good diets. My intention in this chapter is to hopefully plant seeds so you can become more aware, if you are not already, and begin to make better choices for your family too.

In our family, we ourselves are always learning. We believe that health is of vital importance, and this is one of the reasons we choose to naturally grow foods together as part of homeschooling while gaining knowledge on how to improve our choices, and while becoming ever more aware of the possibly harmful choices out there.

Although we find it impossible to apply completely in our own lives, as much as possible we avoid consuming foods from packages, since in most cases such products have typically been factory processed.

For some, food health goes hand-in-hand with not just physical heath but mental health.[20] To our family this would make sense, and it was something Yuko has always been a great example of. She's never been on a weight-loss diet, and I observed how she'd only eat healthy foods, for example when pregnant with our two children, avoiding processed, consuming good foods only, while taking some Chinese herbal remedies to maximize her health. Throughout our lives together, she's always been a great example.

Both our children are growing up to be strong, healthy individuals. Along with our chosen ethos of avoiding processed foods, we discourage them from eating sugar- laden sweets (which they're often offered, say when leaving a restaurant, perhaps in the hope they're enticed to ask us to return).

We share how flour-based foods have much the same effect on the body as eating pure sugars, or other pure carbohydrates, so they shouldn't be a staple diet. Better to eat non-processed carbs such as wholegrain rice with fermented soybeans for breakfast than a bowl of cereal.

It doesn't work for us to stop them from enjoying sweets since this might just make them rebel and eat them in secret later. Instead, we prefer to tell them the reasons why processed foods should be avoided, and suggest if they really want to eat sweets to at least prepare and make them at home, using fresh fruits from our trees and shrubs, eggs from the chicks Akira is responsible for, and soon, honey from our very own bee hives.

Our home's water happens to be from a well of 46m depth. We removed the chlorine dilution/filtering system, preferring instead to consume filtered water, complete with some iron and other natural mineral content. We encourage drinking plenty of water, which, according to Yuko, helps keep our blood clean, and expel toxins from the body.

Our daughter Arina isn't as active as our son Akira. She was never a committed athlete, but loves music, dance and swimming, so we have geared her activities in life at home and outside of it to encompass those.

Our son doesn't need any encouragement to exert his body in pursuit of his latest activities. He has energy to burn! Just the other day when we stopped to have lunch with a young friend, he was soon away running up and down a riverside path, exploring the area, only stopping to chat to locals he'd meet along the way.

Naturally, now being in our early 50s, both Yuko and I aren't as energetic as Akira, but we both realize if we don't maintain our health, we're likely to lose it. Yuko still dances at events and although I have two left feet when it comes to dance, I continue to keep myself trim with daily life, and riding a bicycle at speed when the weather is good.

Knowing (as mentioned elsewhere in this book) that Akira too likes speed on two wheels, I recently spotted a used but beautiful lightweight triathlon racing bicycle suited to his size on an online auction. Over last weekend, I taught him how to fix a puncture on his old bicycle, and encouraged him to clean, polish, and store it away safe from the elements, before we took the contents out of a large box which had finally arrived.

He duly did his homeschool learning activities this morning, before spending much of the day riding his new machine up and down a quiet farm road behind our house at ever faster speeds. Soon, we'll begin riding to build health together. For me, it'll be a lot more fun doing such activities if I can keep him keen to ride, and in turn no doubt he'll encourage me too.

Just this week, with other homeschoolers together, they cut and collected lots of giant bamboo, lashed it together and built a simple raft on which they rode down a shallow river, all while shrieking and giggling excitedly throughout the day.

He's become a keen skateboarder, which also helps keep him fit and energetic, and naturally has now also taken up surfing. This weekend, he designed, built and decorated a simple skim board to use on the beach. Activities such as these help to promote the natural healthy development of a young man who is growing up to be strong, confident, and able.

If anything, as a nine-year-old he has a little too much energy, but we feel this can only be a good thing. It's wonderful to see him continue to develop into a healthy and fit young man.

Of course he has a weakness for things like ice cream, so we let him indulge from time to time, always ensuring he eats good food when at home, but as strange as it may seem, we don't encourage them to consume milk products regularly, preferring nut and other forms of milk for our family as healthier alternatives.[21]

In 2016, one of my oldest friends since childhood shocked me. He'd been one of the healthiest people I'd known; someone very conscious of heath who'd been a vegetarian all of his life.

That day of 2016, he shared a picture of himself four years prior, beside a picture of him now. The difference was startling.

Where despite being a vegetarian all of his life, he'd become a mid-40-something couch potato, now four years later, he'd lost some 25kg (55lbs) and looked much like he had done in our late teens. Super fit and healthy.

He'd taken up competitive marathon running since changing to a whole-plant diet, and shared how now, after four years, he also physically felt 20 years younger. The differences resulting from changing to a vegan whole-plant lifestyle were truly incredible.

Suitably inspired, I too tried to develop into someone on a whole-plant diet. This would have meant no oil in my foods, as whole-plant would mean eating olives, not just the oil squeezed from them.

In the end, although I've now been a vegan for five years, I just couldn't be that strict while living with the other choices Yuko would make for herself, and the children's choices too. They wanted to eat foods they liked, and who was I to dictate what they should eat, just because it would meet my own choices? Instead, Yuko cooks vegan foods and the occasional meat dish at home, and I don't fuss—I can remove the meat, or eat something else. All the while though, I've been a practical example of an alternative and probably healthier choice.

I do recall when we were at St. Christopher School together, my then young friend had tried to become a vegan (the diet offered there was vegetarian, complete with a widely stocked salad bar at every meal) and found himself becoming very skinny!

I would say it really depends on what works for the individual at any given time. Eating a whole-plant diet as a vegan is becoming an increasingly popular life choice for man. It's rare to see an overweight vegan if his choices are healthy and not processed.[22]

While in Okinawa this year, Arina is swimming lots, and is involved in plenty of outdoor activities. Not so many aerobic activities as her brother, she's more gentle and relaxed. Come the winter holidays, we'll take our camper and head to the colder mountain regions, and enjoy winter sports together. This summer we drove in it to beautiful regions of the Japanese countryside and enjoyed holidaying outdoors, which naturally included a lot of swimming in lakes.

Just this weekend, now that the extreme humidity and heat of Japanese summer is finally over, Yuko, Akira and I took to weeding our vegetable garden plots and preparing soil for planting seeds and seedlings. Previously, he'd try to avoid helping with such activities, as he would find gardening boring, but now having gained an interest in our growing flock of chickens, he became more involved. He'd pick out the larvae of insects nesting in the soil, and feed them to the birds.

We maintained conversation among the three of us, and gave him tasks he enjoys more, such as emptying the wheelbarrow into the compost heap. Slowly he's gaining an interest, but sometimes these things develop only if and when the time is right.

With these natural activities, he's naturally also learning without realizing it. We will plant the veggies he likes, and soon our persimmon trees and kiwi will bear fruit. He and I will climb trees to pick them and Yuko will prepare delicious fresh organic smoothies for us to enjoy.

As he grows stronger with each passing year, I will encourage him to take on more responsibilities, and do harder work, whilst also being mindful to teach him how to lift heavy things safely to avoid spinal damage. If we are successful in doing so, I'd love to dig and make a natural swimming pool in our garden that we would build together.

Diving in the morning into a clear gravel pond, where minerals oozing our bodies provide the nutrition for the few aquatic plants, while sharing the water with tadpoles and small frogs, would be a wonderful way for ourselves and our children to wake up and be another great project to complete together.

We're patently aware how children will easily gravitate to watching screens, playing games, or spend hours on social media. By filling their time with more inspiring activities, so far we've been successful in avoiding the pitfalls that come through being glued to a screen. It can be done and I would encourage you and your family to explore the methods of healthy learning that most resonate with you.

As they grow into adolescents, they'll face their own challenges. Our daughter has recently begun to get acne, which can be exacerbated through eating processed foods, so we encourage her to drink plenty of water, eat, sleep, enjoy being outdoors, and avoid worrying. Instead, knowing the best way to influence others is by example, we encourage her to do her best, and follow in Mama's footsteps.

We encourage our children to sleep early and read a good book at bedtime (as opposed to looking at a screen), making sure to have a good, comfortable warm bed. A good night's sleep is important for a growing child; it's when our bodies repair themselves and grow.[23]

In winter, Akira often likes to sleep in our lounge, where there's a wood stove to keep him warm. A good choice, which we'd want for ourselves if only there were a fireplace in our room.

We hope in future what we are trying to pass down to our children as good habits of healthy individuals will in turn become their own personal choices with which to develop further, and may in turn keep them healthy for life.

I hope some of what we do, and shall do in future, may give some inspiration. We include videos of what we get up to in our podcasts, hosted on www.howtohomeschool.life

Health is the major wealth for each of our lives, which must be preserved and maximized. If we can mix good health with a happy way of living that children feel comfortable with, then our chances of instilling good health habits for them are naturally heightened.

11 The Myths of Homeschooling

1. IT'S TOO DIFFICULT TO HOMESCHOOL

"Whether you believe you can do it, or whether you believe you cannot, either way, you're absolutely right!"

- HENRY FORD

"It's too difficult," is just one objection most parents considering homeschooling may initially have. Truth is, if your family is committed, you **can** do it. The biggest hurdle, at first, is to believe in ourselves and in our children.

Yuko, the most gentle woman I have ever intimately known, has in the past declared loudly, "I give up!" We find just a few minutes after such an upset, when we've all calmed down, we're just as committed as ever. Parenting isn't easy at the best of times and homeschooling **is** a learning process. We've learned that to make such declarations doesn't help at all. Yes, we learn from our mistakes.

Our world is changing rapidly around each of us, whether we like it or not. What of schooling during the Coronavirus crisis and the restrictions that are increasingly placed on children, such as enforced mask wearing, face shields, social distancing, no physical contact, vaccines parents may feel they don't need, and later, no doubt more…?

Will our children and we parents be comfortable with such choices becoming a permanent part of their lives, as a byproduct of homeschooling? For some, steps we are being forced to face may be a step too far.

It looks increasingly possible there will be a push toward online schooling in future, with many as yet unknown implications and uncertainties this could introduce.[24] [25]

If online schooling develops with little, if any, direct one-on-one teacher input, how would this affect children as they grow up in years ahead?

From what we are seeing slowly dawn as reality, will we want to gamble that a teacher in an online class of 30-40 children will be able to nurture their inquisitiveness and individual interests? How will children's mental health be further affected if such developments come to be the norm in schools?

These and other questions are what many concerned parents are now asking themselves. You yourself might have many more.

It's of no surprise that increasingly we see more and more concerned parents looking at the alternatives that homeschooling can offer. If free homeschooling is altogether more empowering, inspiring and can ultimately prepare children better for their futures, we hope your family may decide that homeschooling is the most inspiring option. Indeed, this may be one of the most important choices of their lifetimes.

2. I CAN'T TEACH MY KIDS!

A MISTAKE IS ONLY A MISTAKE WHEN I REFUSE TO CORRECT IT.

At first, I began by saying that I didn't have the patience to teach. I had convinced myself that I dislike repeating myself and wasting time. So, I imagined what sort of a homeschooling parent I'd become with such disempowering thinking. Instead, I stopped and asked myself if this line of thinking was really of service to our family's progress, and how could I take responsibility to improve?

Truth is, it was imperative I stopped convincing myself I wasn't good enough and instead concentrated on becoming a lot more patient. I concentrated on improving my skills at inspiring the children through thinking of and looking ahead for fun ways to inspire them to learn.

THERE'S NO TEXTBOOK FORMULA FOR FREEDOM IN HOMESCHOOLING.

My beginner's mistake had been to assume that all children fit into the same jelly mold. We must not forget they're each different individuals, stimulated by entirely different things!

Some of us did well at school, so it's easy to skip along, thinking that education is best left to professionals. Others may feel quite the opposite and didn't do well in a conventional school environment, and therefore lack the confidence to even know where to begin. I implore you. Look deeply at how things are now for your children. To think that schooling now is the same as we parents had it is frankly unrealistic, and we can expect it may be less so in the not too distant future.

There will be many days you'll question free homeschooling just as we did, but as those days go by and you see how your children develop and compare to many others, you'll gain increasingly more confidence and conviction to continue to encourage them to strive in the directions of their chosen passions.

Great learning is when a child is left with more interesting questions after a period of study than they had when they began. To explore and find the answers to such questions and thereby learn is real progress.

If you're present along the way, you'll continue to build a relationship filled with wonderful memories that will greatly help your children toward creating a future they're inspired by. Our task is to ask ourselves what we can do to help to improve how our children learn.

3. I CAN'T AFFORD TO HOMESCHOOL MY KIDS

These Coronavirus crisis times are by far some of the most challenging many of us, including myself, have ever faced. We know other free homeschooling parents who continue to remain committed, despite facing the most difficult challenges. Even single working moms have made homeschooling work by teaming up with other like-minded mothers who take turns to host a small group of children for the day.

Within the homeschooling community we each create around us, our children spend days of the week in alternate nearby locations, with other children to participate in differing activities, study, and socialize together.

For parents with financial challenges, we would strongly recommend creating a local community around yourselves and start to meet other local parents, to see what possibilities may exist around you. You may also find that as you meet other parents, you come to make new and lasting friendships. The socialization you and your kids get from homeschooling is dependent on the commitment you make to having a local community you support and, in turn, are supported by.

Community builds resilience and is an important key to success in homeschooling, so I would urge you to start creating these important connections and relationships.

Speak with relatives, other parents, friends, teachers, and ask if they know anybody personally who might be someone to reach out to. Create a local social media group for homeschooling parents and direct message parents you already know. Share what you have learned in this book. Discuss!

There is no shame in wanting the best for our children. Conventional schooling is looking increasingly less attractive during this Coronavirus crisis, and beyond.

Those who originally planted the seeds of example that inspired us to go on to homeschool ourselves—Christian missionaries—weren't wealthy at all. None of them had their own home. They paid rent like many others and to this day, with their children grown up and moved on, still live by meagre means while continuing to help others.

Not having much income didn't stop them from having many children and homeschooling each and every one of them. Now grown up, some have chosen to go on to universities, some have gone into modelling, and others into careers spanning building work, through ownership of businesses, to high finance.

In several cases, as far as we know, children went into what they were most interested in and our observation is that they are each happy to be following what their interests are. Indeed, many are now homeschooling their own children and continuing to improve on the formula. Some are financially very comfortable, some less so.

"Obstacles are those frightful things you see when you take your eyes off your goals."

- HENRY FORD

So you see, there certainly isn't a requirement to be financially secure in order to homeschool. We'd venture to suggest that homeschooling can be less expensive, since there are no added costs of buying school clothing, trendy shoes, sports gear, satchels, mobile phones to be able to keep up with where they are, driving them to school, lunch money, etc.

Nowadays, having access to a good local library isn't even a requirement, although reading certainly is something to be embraced if a library of reading books is available. Books can be read online, and literature and teaching materials are available for free, such as from https://www.khanacademy.org/

In our case, we have a local Japanese library. We've also chosen to invest in books our children like. The benefit is we can zero in on the books the children are most likely to become engrossed in. With Amazon nowadays able to print on demand and ship books offered from other countries to arrive within days, the world is our proverbial oyster.

For those whose purse strings are tighter, it may be beneficial and entirely possible to build a community around yourself with other like-minded parents. We have done just this, to share our homeschooling materials and ideas, while also giving our children the opportunities to be with other children—both homeschoolers and friends who attend the conventional local schools.

For some parents, careers may until now have dictated that they cannot orient their lives toward spending more time at home, but we believe this is changing globally. More businesses are finding that it may be beneficial for staff to work from home more and spend less time traveling, or even have a need for expensive offices in city centers.

I myself have worked from home for the past two+ decades and fully intend to continue, going forward, even if my current businesses need to change and adapt. For us, our family comes first and the quality of education for our children and what they're inspired toward is our main priority. The rest we will continue to adapt toward so circumstances best meet our needs and not the other way around.

Not least, my example of working from home instills the possibility within our two children where they see and absorb the idea that it really **is** possible to work from home and make a decent living.

Some of us may find ourselves needing to reinvent our careers. Don't look at this as a worrisome mountain, but rather a challenge of love for our children, where love is the most powerful force we can work with. Sometimes, the unknown can be scary, but it will be only if we perceive it as such. Equally, the unknown is an opportunity for learning through mistakes and finding the best solutions. The triumphs of success can be an exciting road or discovery, full of wonder.

Ask yourself if making a real difference to your child's life will be a worthwhile endeavor to you. I so hope your answer is yes and you'll choose to be your child's hero. You can certainly do it if you truly believe in yourself and your child.

4. I DON'T HAVE THE TIME TO HOMESCHOOL

This was one of my classic objections, which even now I sometimes catch myself saying. I only need to look at the passion in our children's eyes into what they're doing, their squeals of delight when playing, or how much they enjoy socializing with others to know there are few better causes to dedicate oneself to in family, especially at times like these.

The world needs leaders and innovators with integrity and love for humanity, not necessarily people who are taught to become salarymen who may typically only follow the narrative they're presented with, living in fear of failure and without questioning the future that may present.

We have a responsibility to these future adults whose care and nurturing we as parents are entrusted with, to share with them the best we can of life. Will we choose to come to the end of our lives and say, "Gosh, I wish I'd worked harder and spent less time bringing up our children?" Of course not. Right?

Yuko gets least time to herself. Every day, I marvel at her energy, drive and sheer determination to provide the very best she can, so we may share a nurturing family life. She gets up at the crack of dawn some mornings to be out in the garden to plant vegetables with Arina, she shops, prepares food and still has time to spend with the children, assisting their studies when needed.

We encourage them to read and write English through innovative ways, inspire them with science experiments or reading colorful science books together. We continually dream up more activities from which we can learn useful skills.

Yuko is often with Arina, helping her prepare for presentations she's working on, and so much more. She drives Akira to classes for swimming and Aikido and Arina to jazz piano, singing, ballet and to attend or perform speeches at environmental events she's invited to speak at.

I acknowledge Yuko and the children daily. I know she doesn't devote much time for herself, so whenever she lets me know she wants to visit friends, or would like to go somewhere, I do my best to make sure that possibility is fulfilled.

The children have simple daily chores, whether it be feeding the chickens and goats, changing their water and bedding, or cleaning our home. Sometimes, they help cook dinner and, on special occasions, I become the chef and spend hours preparing dough and ingredients for pizza, which we now assemble together once the ingredients are all laid out on our kitchen table.

They're expected to tidy and clean up to share in the work we must do, regardless of whether we are tired or not. In these ways, they learn about the many different aspects of family and life, while helping keep the family home presentable, and thereby easing the burden on us parents.

Our home isn't kept as clean or beautiful as we'd like and, occasionally, having many children over, things get worn, broken or damaged. These add character to our lives; such frivolous things are unimportant. Incrementally, day by day, we make progress.

It took years of reminding him, but we no longer find Akira's bicycle abandoned on the driveway, where his earlier machines would get rusty from being rained upon, time after time. Having his own room, he keeps it tidy now. When I find something on the floor that shouldn't be there, I gently remind him—once. If he does it again, I gently remind him the next time.

Arina could prepare and cook a variety of meals at the age of 11 and we encourage our son to learn similarly. He particularly likes getting involved in making sweets and tending to the barbeque. He wants to help me washing our cars, so I find things he can do. He's surprisingly good at cleaning, as he clearly takes an interest and pride in doing a good job.

I observe that, like me, he also has an eye for detail, so he has taken to being responsible for cleaning the interior when we care for the family car. As time continues to fly by, we know they'll leave the roost and find their own ways forward, so these times we share together as a family are to be savored.

To let off steam and relax, now and then Yuko goes out for a walk in the evening. Friday nights we always go out on a date, just the two of us. Often, we end up talking about the two of them and their progress. Spending time together like this is important for our marriage. It's our favorite time of the week!

The kids stay home, watch a movie, or do some craft, or have grown-up friends join them. Arina had always been safety conscious and they know the dangers of fires, etc. We make sure they have no need to cook while we're out, or do anything that might carry risk, and we're only a phone call away, with trusted neighbor friends just next door if there is ever a need.

We look forward to holidays and plan them together, sometimes taking small road trips, or going camping. When they have friends over, we involve them in our family life, and if the kids do things separately, we chat about the activities over a meal.

It's wonderfully rewarding to share these wonderful years of life together, while together building our family memories. Somehow, there's a feeling of older tradition. We avoid having the kids spend time looking at screens, always preferring human interaction. Where they want to read, we will as much as possible facilitate use of books, which they can become more engrossed in.

Where we really want to achieve something, we do our best to make it possible. We're never going to reach the end of our lives and say, "I wish I'd spent less time with the family." Quite the opposite. Enjoy and savor every moment you can.

There is nothing more precious than time.

5. MY OTHER HALF DOESN'T BELIEVE IN HOMESCHOOLING

This may be a difficult challenge some individual parents may face, although in some ways the ultimate decision to homeschool may be made easier during the continually challenging developments of the Covid-19 crisis. Many parents will value higher education as the only way forward. Again, we come to the situation where people, including your own spouse, may only know education in a conventional sense and feel that professionals with a teaching degree are the only ones that can be trusted with our children's education.

If your spouse isn't on board yet, the challenges might be greater. Don't give up without really trying, if homeschooling is what you see your children would be most suited to. They're worth fighting for.

Discuss what a future where children learn through fear of failure through ever more and more testing may result in. Ask yourselves if people you've met in life who are truly passionate about the work they learn is right for them tend to be successful in their fields. Ask yourself if children are being well socialized in the current school systems. Ask yourself if your children know how to be happy.

Research and find examples of success in free homeschooling. There are online groups on Facebook and other social media you can connect with, so reach out! You may be able to meet other parents local to you who are already free homeschooling and able to offer some insight into their own challenges. It's rare that you'll find parents who have successfully been homeschooling their kids for some time, but if you do, chances are they've already seen the results and will be keen to share their experiences.

You'll need the support of your spouse for homeschooling to work, but especially if your child is at school and not easily adapting to the latest changes, you may see good reasons to give homeschooling a try. Your spouse may find it easier to trial homeschooling at first, to make a more permanent decision later.

Failure is an integral part of the path to success and children learn to make better choices through making important ones for themselves from a young age.

If your spouse believes the above and it's your child's strong desire to homeschool, then the choice may be easier. In addition, it is possible you may be persuaded that homeschooling isn't for your child after a decent length of time trial, so be prepared for the unexpected.

Only you, as parent(s) and child(ren), will know if it's right, but if you have bought this book and are thinking of the possibility of free homeschooling, then I hope you'll give it the chance it deserves.

6. DO HOMESCHOOLED KIDS TURN OUT WEIRD?

At the end of her second year at our local primary school, Arina chose to stop attending. She'd made some close friends at school. Her class had been small with only seven or so students.

At first she'd visit one girl who lives just a few minutes away, but over time they drifted apart for no particular reason. Arina was a little saddened at first, but later came to accept it. They still greet one another if their paths cross, but no longer meet up in their own time. Sensing that some people didn't approve or understand her choice, she chose to stop sharing with strangers that she homeschools.

Arina is a very likeable, confident girl with excellent conversational abilities. She can befriend and speak with anybody, often surprising adults at how articulately and maturely she speaks and shares her thinking. She plays well with children of all ages, but says she prefers older girls, even young adults, who she tends to find more interesting to converse with.

Recently, through a growing following after her successes with public speaking, she was invited to a meeting with the mayor, where they discussed the environment for an hour or so. During this time, there were reporters for the prefectural section of a national newspaper.

Although the published report was favorable and described her as a young person with much knowledge, it also mentioned that she doesn't attend school, but instead homeschools. We were surprised to hear comments from our neighbor who had read the article. Arina's ballet teacher also read and shared it with her students and now, it seemed many more knew she was homeschooled.

Arina, being quite sensitive to how people around her feel, noticed a change in how a couple of the others began to treat her. I asked her how she felt and she said that it doesn't really bother her, since they weren't people she'd consider as friends and her genuine friends know of her life, although given the choice, she'd have preferred they didn't know.

When people she doesn't know ask her how school is, she usually says, "Fine." It's just easier to not have to explain each time how she homeschools and what she typically does day to day. She mentions that older people, especially, find it hard to understand the benefits of it and can frown at the idea. None of this means that homeschooling makes our children weird., though. Quite the opposite!

Recently, I took Akira to an enthusiasts' car meet. Despite being only nine years old, within a short time he'd struck up conversation with several people, and proceeded to make them laugh at his wit. He proceeded to make new friendships. Later, these young car owners commented on how amazing this kid was. He already knew so much, and was clearly not afraid to approach anybody and strike up a conversation.

He enjoys making people laugh. By the end of the evening, he'd been offered and accepted a 20-minute ride in a new friend's classic Ferrari (of course, I followed them to ensure he was safe).

A free homeschooled child's early ability to easily strike up new relationships is a skill worth investing time in. All it has taken in our case is the children seeing our example as parents. In our experience, it's more accurate to say that long term, homeschooling can help children become extraordinary, as people who have a history of learning through passion and fun.

Conversely in this world, where conventional education has become more and more about memorization, where human relationships are increasingly eroded into online and virtual ones, surely there are benefits to developing communicational skills through direct conversations that can be so much more diverse and prevalent in a free homeschooled environment.

Children get entire days of playing with friends, in natural and open surroundings. They build better relationships through playing without a set time limit for break times. It's evident in who they are as confident young people that homeschooling doesn't make them insular. Quite the opposite as we've witnessed with our kids and other homeschoolers.

This isn't to say that every homeschooler will grow up to be a self-confident individual. Just as in conventional school, some will choose to hide behind shyness, or awkwardness, while growing up. It is beneficial for children to realize that shyness isn't a condition, but a choice that we make subconsciously to avoid encounters we may find uncomfortable. One task as parents is to lead by example—how to be with others, by being who we are, freely. Children learn much, much more from observing us than we typically notice.

Neither myself nor Yuko choose to be shy people; we're warm, keen to share valuable conversations and are happy to help others along the way wherever we can. We have no doubt our children have seen this since infancy. Sometimes, with adults they're a bit cautious, but they soon lose their inhibitions and become playful and chatty. Sometimes, on occasions they are even disruptive, having enthusiasm to join conversations we're having with other adults.

We take the learning of socialization one step at a time.

Children also learn socialization from being with people other than family. In our experience, this has so far worked best from being with older children and adults, but that's not to say they don't benefit from being around younger children. We've watched Arina play with younger children in charming ways, where she's really dedicated to sharing their time together, almost as if she's reliving her own childhood, and this is also heart-warming to see. As a father I can't help thinking that someday she'll be a wonderful mother, much like her own mum.

When I was a child, I told myself I would never forget how to be a child and how to play. My youngest siblings are 11 and 13 years younger than me, but by the time I was in my early 20s, I'd begun to forget about some of the things I liked when I was their age. In turn, when Akira was born, I realized I'd forgotten how to play as a child. This is something I'd like our children never to forget by the time they have their own. In my mind, a good way to reinforce their childhood playing abilities is to continue encouraging both of them to play with children of all ages, young and old.

The most free and inspiring young adults are those who have truly lived and enjoyed their childhoods.

12 The Digital Pacifier

READING MAKES US SMART. SMARTPHONES MAKE US STUPID.

I look at our son aged nine, and although for his first year I was concerned he wasn't making good progress, now I look back and see in fact he's gained so much it's astounding. He speaks and reads two languages. He has lots of natural knowledge, only a small proportion of which he gleaned from his classes, before choosing to start homeschooling. Through his own interests, he can tell me much more than I know about insects and crustaceans.

He, like so many natural children today, was distracted and very energetic, unable to sit still in class, before he started homeschooling. I look back at myself as a child and recall how I'd always been energetic and how I too was easily distracted and prone to daydreaming, just as he has been. Such memories though, remind me of how valuable those years were, even though I hadn't been fully paying attention to what the teachers were trying to instill in me.

I taught him to read English, and through this year reinforced his interest. He's learned lots about racing go-carts and is reading adult instruction/discussion on racecraft. He wants to be fastest, and will read books about it and understand if that's what it takes.

Books are the seeds prepared by others for the growth of our knowledge.

The wisest people we know have, since childhood, read many books and tend to be the most eloquent in their choices of words.

We cannot judge a person for the titles and authors' writing they have contemplated, but we may come to find their opinions formed as more authoritative and interesting as we find ourselves enjoying conversations with them.

Reading of books for themselves clearly allows children to exercise and continue to develop their imaginations. Stop and consider what they can absorb. As they read further, they stand to naturally develop not just their vocabulary, punctuation, grammar, and spelling, but writing style, and articulation. Last, but not least, children can fuel their passion for a bottomless depth of knowledge.

Edison's childhood story and so many others you will undoubtedly come across may serve to remind each of us that we must be patient. We must avoid pushing or nagging our child to improve his reading, but rather inspire him continuously through fun means. If one doesn't work, be patient and try another tack. We may be trying too early.

In his own time, he may discover for himself that reading and absorbing new knowledge will open doors to an infinite world of discoveries. Enchantment comes from learning new things and going on to create more as he is inspired. As we each develop our reading, seeds for knowledge are continuously planted, sprouting more questions and a yearning for answers.

Using animated books and subjects I know he's fascinated with, our son continues developing steadily. Some years prior, our daughter became a voracious reader in two languages herself.

Again looking back, I remember poring over maps when I was younger with an interest in learning where the subjects of stories were from and what their lives might have been like, their climates, cultures, and more.

Today, it's all too easy just looking it up online. We can just type a name into our preferred search engine. A laptop computer on which I sit here writing, despite being small and light enough to be easily portable, is one of the most powerful tools available. Our smartphones have also become incredibly powerful machines.

There are valid arguments for not reading physical books and, instead, finding content online.

Electronic media is often free, more "environmentally friendly" and there is a **lot** more content out there. If we search, we will find many glowing reports explaining how learning online is the embracing of tomorrow's world.

Amazon sells Kindle format books. We can watch videos of authors reading their own books, or even hear a publication being read while we do something else, such as driving.

I remember the advent of the Third Industrial Revolution when the internet started to become prevalent in the late 80s. I recall asking my more tech-savvy university friends just starting out their careers what "email" was, just before I was introduced to emails at work.

As responsible parents, surely we want our children to have early access to these latest technologies which will be ever more developed and present in their future lives, not just as they grow up, but throughout their professional careers? Our son is very interested in robots and, therefore, programing. Knowing computers are to be an integral part of the lives of adults in future, even more than today, we have enrolled him in weekly robot programing classes.

Therein lies the dilemma. You see, with books, our children generally have far less probable distractions than when reading content from a tablet, or even a PC. The notifications that audibly and visually signal that something is now awaiting us are designed to steal our attention, and that's only the beginning of it.

We only need take a look at some of Silicon Valley's top executives' and sometimes even ex-executives' warnings to begin to understand some of the dangers that threaten our children's innocence and wellbeing. Should we let them delve too deeply into what's possible online? Do you feel this may sound a bit far-fetched? You'd be forgiven for thinking so, just as I did when I first began contemplating the idea.

Perhaps I had a head start, having seen how detrimental computer games were for a younger boy's development as I watched him grow up. By the time he was an adult, this young man was so hopelessly addicted that he flunked his first year at an Ivy League college and was expelled. The reason? He was unable to stop himself spending nights playing games and his days sleeping, instead of attending lectures.

Back then, around 2006, social media as we know it today barely existed, but I had seen how dangerous computers and gaming had already become. Games and the internet have gotten a lot more powerful and addictive since.

YouTube is full of great videos with instructions that are useful: There are excellent drawing tutorials, videos on how to conduct science experiments and infinitely interesting topics abound. Facebook is a great way for our friends and relatives to keep in touch. Google makes our lives so much easier, and our children seem to get much enjoyment from TikTok.

But Tristan Harris, an ex-executive from Silicon Valley with a moral conscience warns:

"If you aren't paying for the product, then you are the product." [26]

Facebook, Instagram, YouTube, Snapchat, Twitter, TikTok, Pinterest, Reddit, LinkedIn, to name a few, all operate on the same business model: These platforms are engineered to regularly send notifications that entice the user to check what's happening.

Once your child hops on to a platform, her algorithmic feed, guided by her browsing history, aims to successfully entice her to stay on the service for maximized periods of time. The platform will continuously suggest enticing content and regularly send her "ping" alerts when others respond.

"The gradual, slight, imperceptible change in your own behavior and perception—that is the product, the only product they sell."

- JARON LANIER[27]

All social media platforms monitor user actions. They know which sites our child visits. Platforms record the news we read, where we find it and can thereby discern with ever increasing accuracy what each of our views and opinions are.

Navigational apps follow our every journey, knowing when we stop to eat, fill up, or meet someone.

They record every move. Each of these platforms build AI algorithms that predict our every action and move. The aim of their game is whichever company can best predict our next action, thought or emotion, ultimately wins the largest advertising revenue (currently, this would be Google).

I must apologize if I am coming across as overdramatic, but this is not a trifling matter.

As social media is used as a free means of communication, children today are increasingly finding themselves to be victims of cyber bullying, which can be vicious, since the audiences can be larger and the intensity of hurtful remarks on a chat group can be continuous. The bullying and shaming, as well as sexual harassment, doesn't necessarily stop when all the schoolchildren go home. It can get worse from then on and continue onward, the next day, and beyond.

It's not uncommon for nude pictures to be requested by boys from girls who may be attracted to them, or even vice-versa. When the relationship ends, the pictures don't disappear, and can be used against the interests of the person(s) featured.

Coronavirus crisis aside, and its repercussions, there's no wonder, even before the current challenges, we were already seeing a gradual but alarming rise in mental health and anxiety issues in young children, especially girls, all the way up to adults in their mid-20s.

Moral outrage gets social media attention. Meanwhile, there is really no impetus for social media to police and stop this sort of behavior on most private chat groups. Could it be that such actions are beneficial for such platforms, since they keep users online for longer and thereby generate more advertiser revenue from maximizing audience ratings?

Certainly, large social media audiences generate huge advertising revenues, which in turn provide handsome shareholder dividends, but should our lives and how they're affected boil down to a focus purely on maximizing financial profit?

And what about the sharp rise in pedophile activity which has been growing ever since children started getting online, to innocently meet existing friends and seek to find new friends?

In so many ways, social media today pulls children away from their families and real friends, but it is a business and technology that clearly shows it doesn't care about the "user," but about its shareholders' bottom line.

"We have moved on from a tools-based technology environment to an addiction and manipulation-based technology environment, which uses our psychology against us."

- TRISTAN HARRIS

Around our own homeschooling community, there are parents who give their children liberty to spend as much time as they want playing games and being online. We observe that such children are more likely to be addicted and thereby choose not to participate in fun activities with other children.

Some teenagers today will refuse to eat a family meal without a smart device to scroll through. When we consider that a family meal is one of the most opportune times we connect with one another, to share and discuss what is happening in our lives, to have that time hijacked may be a great loss.

Given the opportunity, social media will rule children's lives, as they seek online approval through likes, loves, thumbs-up and new followers. Through these means, social media is designed to first seduce, then demand and even unknowingly manipulate our children's minds, while indirectly but very effectively distracting them from natural learning.

With ever incredibly large amounts of income and growth, Big Tech's power is anticipated to continue advancing exponentially, to predict and distract more of our children's lives as the algorithms (AI) learn how to better influence and addict them with momentary doses of dopamine to keep them interested.

News media sells our attention to advertisers, where the ability to influence our perception is their goal, but that goal is being redesigned and developed constantly, as social media goals continue to be met and surpassed.

YouTube makes money by propagating unregulated messages to the widest captive audience for the best prices, whilst with YouTube for kids, protections and regulations are no longer a hindrance, compared to the TV program regulations that many of us older generations grew up to accept as necessary.

Now social media platforms are targeting our children, at ever younger ages, in the full knowledge that if they can captivate their attentions at a young age, the platforms will stand to breed intimacy for life, to turn our children into proverbial cash cows.

For the first time in a generation, many young children care whether others in their virtual tribe approve of them or not. Social approval becomes a condition for them if we let it seep into their lives without their awareness.

"Fake brutal popularity."

- CHAMATH PALIHAPITIYA[28]

This is a very bad vicious circle we're living in and it's important to know the truth. Since the introduction of social media appearing on smartphones, anxiety and depression, as well as teenage suicides, have surpassed a 100-200% growth rate and continue to climb alarmingly.

The rights and privileges of incredibly large Big Tech companies are protected through existing legislation, supported and steered by powerful lobbies. Facebook lobbies governments and negotiates its terms, whilst in such huge multinational corporations, highly paid lawyers and accountants work out the most favorable ways for these platforms to pay the least taxes.

Such a sadly common Big Tech trajectory undermines rights and human freedoms. Unchecked of the need to operate with integrity, as now the world's wealthiest industry, a whole young generation is being unknowingly coerced into people who are generally anxious, fragile, easily depressed, and much less comfortable with taking risks. Trends such as these began to develop around 2011-2013, as Facebook grew exponentially through use of clever AI algorithms.

"Taking driver's tests or going out on dates is dropping dramatically for the youngest generations on social media."

- JONATHAN HAIDT

There are laws that criminalize hard drugs, which are dangerous enough to destroy people's lives. Yet, here we are in an age where powerful platforms are openly intent on controlling people's perceptions. This carries on to such a finite amount that adverts are being used to influence the future choices of young uncertain adults about which political party to vote for at a general election. Such manipulation is possible through individually targeted influences of an eligible voter's opinions.

Currently, by leading us on with a different story for each of us to believe as perceived reality, social media is on an uncontrolled course to destroy the very fabric and freedoms of society that represent what many of us know must remain as inalienable rights.

Where those of us reading this chapter absorbed many experiences during our childhoods at home, which in turn provide a blueprint with how we are with our children, consider what can happen for children who grow up with a smartphone or tablet as the babysitter or digital pacifier.

Big Tech knows this is happening, but sadly it's not something they can easily control, not least when the primary focus is on making obscene amounts of wealth for stockholders.

Many executives working in Big Tech are aware of the dangers I am sharing here, but there is no one person to blame. Big Tech executives are most aware of the dangers their social media platforms subject children to, but they're not the ones able to make life-changing decisions affecting billions.

Many Silicon Valley parents insist that their own children are not exposed till as late as possible. There are private schools catering to such families that won't allow children access to smartphones and tablets. Many Silicon Valley parents insist there must be no smart devices in their households either.

Indeed, these concerned tech industry parents, some of whom were homeschooled during their own childhoods, will see the wisdom of letting their own children learn through their greatest interests, even at home, and avoiding brutally addictive smartphones and social media.

If such tech industry parents seek to avoid letting their children fall prey to the ever growing dangers of social media, surely this is why some of us may decide to follow their lead? After all, it's not often we get great advice from the top of the most successful companies in the world.

It's our choice: Either we and our children become fully aware of these dangerous platforms and how detrimentally they can affect our lives, or we stand to lose much that we value today—before we even realize it's gone.

• The notion to delete all the social media we are exposed to would be wonderful. For some brave and committed parents, this may be the right choice. For most others, such as my own family, we can foresee that social media has already become an important part of our work and careers.

- I recently sat with our two children and together we watched the Netflix movie *The Social Dilemma*, so they'd have some awareness of the dangers they're subjecting themselves to each time they watch another suggested YouTube video. Afterward, we discussed what they'd understood.

- Although even before watching the movie they were rarely found swiping a tablet, smartphone or computer trackpad (as I write, neither of our children have their own, we intend to avoid such until as late as possible), the danger is that as they become more independent, they will be increasingly distracted by these platforms.

- We can change how we relate to apps, but we instill the importance in our children to take charge, rather than being blindly sucked in.

- Here are some suggestions you may want to consider with your child (or even for yourself), perhaps after watching the movie, but most importantly, before he gets too engrossed and consumed by it:

  * Switch off **all** notifications from installed apps.

  * Delete all unnecessary apps.

  * No exposure to social media till senior high school age, or adulthood, if possible.

  * Work out a daily screen-time budget with your child (this includes playing computer games and watching movies or TV).

  * Always avoid commenting, liking or any interactions while consuming social media (avoids the app learning what the user is stimulated by).

  * If children cannot resist social media, encourage them

to be content creators rather than consumers.

* Always make own choices, avoid "clicking" on suggestions.

* Make a point of not looking at your phone when with someone else (*your children are also watching YOU!*)

* None of your family should be looking at screens when at a meal with others.

* All devices out of each bedroom at a fixed time every night.

* Don't use Google, but a search engine such as duckduckgo.com which (at the time of writing) doesn't store search histories.

• I realize some of the above may seem hard, if not impossible.

• I spend much less time on social media these days, from having understood the darker nature and intentionality. Personally, I now find social media repulsive and being aware of how addictive it can be, I avoid it.

• We continue to entice our children with activities they personally find more interesting. Despite both our children knowing of social media's existence, Akira is happiest when he's tinkering with or building something, and our daughter will gravitate toward activities in art.

• Occasionally, we'll find them engrossed, looking at one of our smartphones, and tell them to stop, reminding them that smartphones make us stupid. Nobody likes being taken advantage of. When reminded, they stop.

• **Nobody will reach the end of their life and regret not having spent more of their time on social media.**

13 Free Homeschooling, The Coronavirus Crisis and The Great Reset

Image credit: Arina Varella-Cid

What I am about to share will undoubtedly seem negative at first, but please bear with me. The end of this chapter offers great positivity that we are unlikely to find elsewhere.

There is a need to present the truth first, to share the problems which humanity is currently facing before presenting what I see as the best solution for planting empowering seeds of growth within our children.

Globally, 2020 was a shocking and very sad year for many young people. Those whose governments allowed children to return to school have found their studies severely disrupted during the first year of the Coronavirus crisis. Mask wearing has become the new norm for countless children throughout the world, and as more Coronaviruses are "discovered",[29] some may be forgiven for anticipating more measures are to be rolled out. We may even experience lockdowns again.[30]

Here in Japan, despite there being no legal mandates or lockdowns (it's forbidden in Japan's constitution to impose curfews of any kind),[31] children from primary school and up have been required to wear a mask since almost the beginning of the pandemic, and to this day, despite (at the time of writing) now nearly 50% of the population having been vaccinated, masks continue to be voluntarily worn by the vast majority of Japanese, including infants.[32]

On a global First World scale, despite a clear understanding by many that young people are the least likely to be in any immediate danger from Covid-19, many now expect top-up vaccines. Pfizer is now developing a pill that supposedly reduces severity when taken daily.[33]

Is this never-ending mask wearing, social distancing, PCR testing, vaccination and other pharmaceuticals, likely followed by Covid-19 IDs and more, the future we want our children to live into?

Viruses, by nature, will usually burn themselves out within two years, as the threshold of herd immunity is reached.[34] Many parents feel their children's right to an education and freedoms are being seriously undermined.[35]

Parents of children who have had no choice but to stay at home and be isolated from their school friends became increasingly concerned at how much time their children have been spending online.[36] In an effort to respond to government directives, schools and teachers have begun to take to online methods of teaching. Most have found that children's pace of learning has slowed down, and their education has been severely affected.[37]

It isn't only academic learning that has been negatively affected. Children who are isolated from others report boredom, sadness, depression, irritability and, in some cases, even suicidal thoughts.[38]

Without social interaction, physical contact and positive emotional stimulation, children have unnaturally lost an important part of their social development. It is a sad consequence that some have succeeded in taking their own lives.[39]

Speaking with friends via Zoom or other means during lockdowns has been a pale substitute for energetic play, discovery, laughter, and fun that was perfectly normal before. Many parents sympathize with their children's pain and desperation to be with their friends.

In some countries, where schools have reopened, teachers report that returning children are more prone to arguing and displaying irritability. This may have much to do with having been isolated for months, instead of being able to socialize freely with their friends.

Even now, as some return to school, many children are unable to see one another's facial expressions. They each breathe stuffy air, to reinhale bacteria the lungs naturally expelled from their bodies.

Despite the understanding that masks have limited effectiveness and that there may be health and brain development risks associated with long-term use, it's expected by many that directives will continue to require children to wear masks nonetheless.[40]

Such measures aren't legal requirements in many cases, but social pressure can be such that many parents don't speak out in their children's defense or simply choose to comply—without question.

Even with a vaccine, people are convinced they must continue to abide by rules, and the increasing likelihood is that top-up boosters will be rolled out and members of the public be coerced into taking them, and complying with vaccine proof/ID requirements, as time passes. Such directions, resultant social costs and erosion of freedoms for future generations continue to become ever less logically attractive as time goes by.[41]

The overall long-term effect we may agree we are seeing develop globally is the erosion of human relationships on an incalculable scale. Many children are not able to see their grandparents, other relatives, or friends. Many parents nowadays no longer go to work, but instead work from home.

The youngest children (who began forming their first memories during 2020), see the fear people now have of contact with one another. These may form memories which they may carry into adulthood. Where we live, here in Japan, nearly everybody chooses to wear a mask when out in public.

I often wonder what the smallest children perceive of this dystopian normality and am saddened for them in what they're unaware they're missing. Some of them may never come to know.

If children continue to be led and conditioned to be afraid, or uncomfortable with being near others, unable to see facial expressions, is their greatest wealth of life not threatened?

How any of us adults have made progress in life is through the strength of the relationships we have built around us. As each of us grows up, we keep snapshots of times we felt something special. It could be memories walking with grandparents, an early romance, or doing something unforgettable with someone special. Adolescence is a time we develop emotionally. We experience building close relationships with others.

We parents may have experienced poignant events such as seeing or hearing beautiful art, socializing as a group, playing on crowded beaches, attending concerts with our closest friends, feeling touched by live music, and many other experiences. Most of such memories, except perhaps just a few, included a relationship with another person.

Almost every important business transaction or deal is interpersonal, and whenever any of us has built a thriving business or a successful, happy career, that has been facilitated through the strength of relationships we have with others around us.

At the last hour of our lives, if our minds are conscious, it will be the love and relationships that we have with family and close friends that will be the most valuable of all. The strongest of which not all the money in the world could buy or replace.

Such is the strength of relationships that it makes the worst pains of incurable illness bearable. The greatest wealth that comes from relationships is something we must not only keep close to our hearts, but encourage our children to embrace, experience and understand.[42]

At the time of writing, we are still in the midst of the Coronavirus crisis which is a far more powerful persuader than even climate change. A virus panic works immediately, where conversely, climate panic follows with a lengthy time lag.

Some of us have seen the costly unsustainability during 2020 and beyond, of closing down businesses both small and large, and the repercussions that countries are likely to suffer by taking on unrepayable debt.

At this stage, we have long since passed logical ways of stabilizing economies of the world. Helicopter Money, considered to be the last resort, was just the start, and money continues being printed without limit, to support and to buy whatever is considered necessary.

Even before the very start of the Coronavirus crisis, stock markets were artificially hyper-inflated with over $2.5 trillion, created by the Federal Reserve, while simultaneously, most of the world began to find its freedoms and, in many cases, the ability to make a stipend income be curtailed.

This amounts to the wealthiest billionaires and elites continuing to destroy the middle class, while enrichening themselves on a massive scale. Make no mistake, the middle class is being systemically destroyed.[43]

The justification we are presented with to explain all the decline is Covid-19, a disease which is faceless and bears no personal responsibility. Some of us look beyond the pandemic to where humanity is being steered: The Great Reset.[44]

Many of the world's leaders are embracing as the future the supposedly inevitable consequence of the Fourth Industrial Revolution.[45] Where the Third Industrial Revolution occurred in the '80s, with the widescale adoption of PCs, then the Internet around a decade later, the fourth is about artificial intelligence, and how robots will replace many of the jobs that are currently in the process of vanishing. The Fourth Industrial Revolution is upon us.

To illustrate: During the first few months of 2020's lockdowns where many non-essential businesses were shut down, Amazon's sales grew by 26%.[46] Amazon openly predicts that within 10 years, they won't need any human fulfillment staff. To remain competitive and in a bid to survive, other retailers are following suit.

All around us, in supermarkets, stores, even airport check-ins, we see faceless AI replacements, where previously there was human interaction, while no substitute jobs are being made available for redundant staff.

We've seen social media grow to hold such power that it can steer government policy where in fact, if government were truly there to serve the people, social media wouldn't be allowed to do as it pleases. Social media has grown to the extent that its income dwarfs the annual GDP of sizable countries.[47]

Such global entities negotiate deals with government at the highest levels and are thereby able to favorably reduce corporate taxes.

Central banks continue to create money *ad infinitum*, regardless of historic events where such inflation of money supply has led to currency collapse.[48] It's as if central banks around the world are preparing for such to happen, so they can replace our current fiat money with a new digital global currency. This is currently a theoretical idea, but how long until we see the biggest financial crash of all?[49]

We look at Japan, one of the world's most technologically advanced countries, and see children wearing masks, weary of school, but lacking of a better choice, attending, and being educated in the same ways as their parents were, training to become hard-working salarymen. Trained not to question and challenge authority, here, children are conditioned to do as they're told.[50]

Their grandparents enjoyed such jobs for life and enjoyed a decent income. Their parents have held stable jobs for years, but the buying power of their incomes has steadily declined, as have their pensions. This trend is set to worsen, as the continuing effects of inflation dawn as reality for each of us.

By the time young Japanese schoolchildren of today are grown up, many of the jobs their relatives found easy to get as they left school may no longer even exist as jobs for humans.

Similar scenarios, with minor differences, occur in other countries around the world. Children's education is being systematically dumbed down, while a great many parents who are aware continue to watch things change.

World leaders are expectant that many jobs will disappear, and that much of the workforce will need to be retrained. Even then, new jobs may simply not be available. Robots don't need rest. They can work 24/7 and don't need pensions. They can be made obsolete at the press of a button. So much easier than with human staff.

World leaders are clearly in unison when they speak about the Great Reset for humanity:

A reset, where everything about us is known and recorded,

through digitized IDs.

A future where we "will own nothing and be happy."

A future where money is digitized, and in some cases provided as a basic income, on the proviso of conformity.

The Great Reset is not intended as the end of globalization. On the contrary, it is globalization centralized and without competition, where the intention is that humanity will be forced to do as we are told, and not as we are inspired.[51]

I feel truly sorry for those who don't yet see the directions that this relatively small group of the wealthiest, most powerful, best connected, but ultimately unelected people appear to be intent on steering the world toward.[52]

Although I believe some of these members truly think they're doing good, they're steering us toward a future where brutal globalism and information technology threatens to control how we live. Some see the end goal as tantamount to the enslavement of humanity.

Of course, if you watch the bought and paid for mainstream media, by design, you won't yet be aware of the Great Reset. The last thing the elite want is for people to be aware of what they plan, but if we follow the money, the truth usually becomes clear.[53]

If you're interested, you can buy Klaus Schwab's books and read for yourself, although I wouldn't want to recommend or help support his work. The Great Reset is clearly not a secret and neither mainstream nor global social media corporations would dare question its narrative.

World leaders and globalist elites believe the Great Reset is just what we must implement regardless, and if we have been observing carefully, they're vocally supportive of it, touting the phrase "Build Back Better" in their speeches.

Some whistleblowers will do their best to expose what is planned, some believe that international lawyers at work will soon stop this, and the many injustices that are increasingly becoming exposed to return humanity to how it was before. Some believe the mainstream news as irrefutable fact, and some believe a mix of all of the above, or don't know what to believe.

Nobody can know for sure what has really taken place behind the scenes, and what will happen going forward. I prefer to respect everybody else's opinion to be just as valid as my own, while continuing to do my best to help others.

I believe we're all on the same side. And ultimately, all of us want the same.

I want a beautiful future for my children and for all of humanity. What sort of future do you want?

Klaus Schwab is the founder of the World Economic Forum, which usually meets in Davos each year. Mr. Schwab is the leading proponent of the Great Reset. The WEF is an annual gathering of world leaders, royalty, CEOs of the world's largest corporations, and the world's most powerful billionaires.

The 2020 event convened nearly 3,000 participants from 117 countries, including 53 heads of state.[54] They fly in by private jet and have no problem with membership fees ranging up to $620,000 per year, where chalets can cost a mere $150,000 weekly. As a CEO, to be eligible as a WEF attendee, your multinational corporation's value should exceed $5 billion.

At this event, these largely unelected elites rub shoulders, discuss, imagine and plan policies for how the world is to be governed and how government lobbying is to be steered.

It is no secret that in 2019's WEF November conference, Event 201, a carefully detailed study of how a pandemic called SARS Cov-2 would affect the world was openly presented to attendees.[55] Whether by sheer luck, or design, it would appear these elite were informed three months in advance what would happen when Covid-19 was declared a pandemic, just four months later. In knowing the agenda, they'd be able to strategize in order to take financial advantages.

Coronavirus is the convenient vehicle through which the world is being shuffled toward the Great Reset, while those without knowledge of what is planned grapple with confusion and fear coming into their homes through TVs.

The Topic for the 2021 Event, which was postponed, was the 'Great Reset'.[56] These 3,000 powerful individuals intend to present, discuss and decide how policies are to be implemented, and how they intend to continue to lead the world, or rather, continue to keep the masses controllable, whilst governments proceed with preparations for how they perceive the world is to be run.

Klaus Schwab, himself not even an elected official, states that a return to normality is fiction. In his writings, co-authored with Thierry Malleret, the authors admit that Covid-19 is *"one of the least deadly pandemics the world has experienced in the last 2000 years."* They have cleverly but grotesquely disfigured it into a pretext for unprecedented social and economic change.

We must remember that what is being carefully planned has not reached a foregone conclusion. 7 billion humans inhabit the earth and as we become aware, as more and more are, the control of humanity through fear and confusion becomes unfeasible.

Each and every one of us 7 billion humans was born and introduced to this wonderful world as a beautiful, small, but yet helpless and innocent miracle. Our parents cared for us in the best ways they could, just as we each care for and love our own children. Some of our ancestors lost their lives for our freedom.

We must firmly remind leaders of governments that they are legally obliged to serve humanity, not the other way around, and they are not elected to serve those who lobby and seek to direct them. We must hold each and every one of our elected leaders to account for what they have been doing.

Regardless of how privileged or not we may be, each of us can access the greatest wealth of all, through which all other lesser versions of wealth are created: relationships.

Relationships are, in fact, more valuable than financial wealth; indeed, as I have said before, it is through relationships that we create all financial wealth.

Where relationships are currently being eroded through restrictions, mask wearing, social distancing, fear, and through perceived differences of opinion, we each have a choice to make: We can either continue to wait for the Great Reset to be implemented, or we can imbue in our children the power of love and relationships that cannot be unlocked from their hearts.

From within, strength is built from the ability to create and continue to strengthen relationships with others. And where we choose, with God. Some of us embrace God, and some of us choose not to.

I am not here to persuade others to believe as I do. Your beliefs and opinions are yours and each of our opinions are as valid as any others. I cannot help but see God's work all around me. Nature has too much intelligence in its beauty and design not to have had a designer, but that's just my belief. Your interpretation is just as valid. I understand the power that is borne of choice.

We must first each see what is happening for ourselves if we are to understand and know the truth about the dangers that much of humanity appears yet unaware of, and we must share it. Through the power of knowledge, we can thereby work out ways to naturally build community with one another, and thereby create resilience and later, growth and fair prosperity.

Most importantly, we must build happiness, which is built from surrounding ourselves with great relationships. Community is naturally how we create strength and resilience around us.

LOVE IS THE ACCEPTANCE OF ANOTHER, WITHOUT CONDITION.

Love is the most powerful force of all.

Love is what I have with my family, and it strengthens me.

Love, when in abundance, continues to grow, spread and make a difference for others without expectation of anything in return, and so those of us who have the power of love in our hearts are able to spread it. With the power of love, humanity can seed the growth of happiness for all.

I am blessed to have personally experienced the existence of another dear friend's spirit, when he showed his soul still exists just a couple of minutes after his body died.

Knowing when this brief flicker of a flame we call life is over that our souls do not die is a very comforting gift. It is a source of immeasurable strength in the face of the gravest challenge.

Knowing and not having to believe is a comfort for which I am deeply thankful to my dear friend James.

In the podcasts I look forward to creating, as this book is published (www.howtohomeschool.life) I will generously share in detail the experience I had the night dear James died and hope through sharing and discussing that event I can in turn empower you. (*In the last chapter, I will invite you to join our email list and free homeschooler's community.*)

All around the world, if we've observed closely, we can see that nature is in rapid decline. Without cohabitation with nature, we, as natural beings, may soon cease to exist. Yet humanity remains blind, as we continue to destroy nature. Nature always strives to return to how it was designed to sustain us, for a world where we are sustained in health, coexistence, and in harmony with nature.

Our health depends on the nature we consume. We can understand that most of the diseases we are afflicted with result from the poor-quality foods we consume.

Why do we attempt to destroy the living organism that supports our very existence?

Now I have briefly shared some of what I have come to understand as important, from decades of daily study into what is happening around the world and how it affects us, I say: There is no point in dwelling on the negatives and the wrong in what we see is being used against humanity.

Although all parents and children should make ourselves aware of the truth, we are far more empowered when we are making a difference.

The intentionality to make a difference comes through being loved, nurtured and encouraged to be the best example of ourselves.

If each of us are aware we (including our children) are headed in dangerous directions, want to make a difference, we must concentrate on reversing the current and foreseeably continuing destruction of human relationships.

The most effective way to fight evil and inspire others is not with evil. It is with good.

With love we can restore, enhance and create relationships, to thereby contribute to building a lasting and true wealth for humanity. This is a task of far bigger importance than ourselves. If we focus on the scale of what is at stake and with love in our hearts, we become unstoppable. In turn, others see us and are inspired. Our children see us.

If you've seen your young child's happiness decline during lockdown and other changes described at the beginning of this chapter, then perhaps now is the time to discuss and understand what he'd like to do.

Most people who attend school never get to see how brilliant they can be. They don't find teachers who believe in them. They become convinced they're not good enough and do what is required of them; they unconsciously become afraid of failure.

The children who have the best chances may be those who are homeschooled with love, empowerment and understanding of what's important in life. They have enhanced their learning and understanding through focussing on the things their minds are captivated by throughout their early childhood. Theirs will be the choice of becoming what they want, having focused on developing their unique talent(s).

With a love for life, an unshakable self-belief and commitment to their visions, our children can inspire many others and thereby have a better chance to in turn make a real and inspiring difference for humanity during their lifetimes.

I am inspired to make a difference and not live a life of fear. When this one is over, I intend to look back, marvel and celebrate the joy I have enjoyed together with others, in the face of fear we, together, have cast away.

NOW and THE FUTURE

——

14 Seven Steps to Free Homeschool Success

Clearly, it is most important for you and your child(ren) to first really consider and discuss if free homeschooling is what your family wants to take on.

Assuming you've been through all the chapters of this book so far, you should by now have a clear idea of what free schooling, with learning focused on passion, is all about and know if it's something you want to try.

Remember also that you can immerse yourselves slowly into free homeschooling, even while your child continues to do other in-person or online schooling if that is your choice.

Free homeschooling is, of course, different from state school schooling. Our tutor, Furuyama San, with decades of experience of homeschool tutoring, told us before we began with our own that we should expect the children would need time to adjust and "unschool" themselves. One month per year they've attended school is the norm although this is only a rough guide; every child is different.

Once you and your child have decided you want to be free homeschoolers, the following are seven of the first steps we would recommend considering, researching and preparing, before beginning.

1. INFORM YOURSELVES OF LEGAL REQUIREMENTS FOR HOMESCHOOLING

In the U.S. homeschooling is regulated by the state rather than the federal government. You will therefore need to look into state regulations specifically. For other countries, you'll need to comply with national requirements.[57]

Contact your local education authority or go to their local office and obtain written information on the current regulations. Speak with someone there who is knowledgeable, obtain their contact information if possible, and explain what your intentions are.

Especially during these difficult times, the staff there may empathize with your concerns that may have first led your family to consider homeschooling, and be willing to go out of their way to help you. Ask if they know how you might be able to contact other local parents who are also considering homeschooling while you're there. You'll never know what help you may get without asking.

Some American states consider homeschooling to be the equivalent of private school. Some states have specific homeschool statutes, and some states have no homeschool regulations at all.

Don't assume that just because legal jargon and stated requirements may be confusing and difficult to understand at first that they are hard to comply with. Other established local homeschooling families you'll meet are likely to be keen to help you and may offer guidance in understanding the legal requirements.

You must be sure to understand the legal requirements for the most up-to-date and accurate legal information pertaining to the country and region you have residence in.

2. FIND LOCAL HOMESCHOOLER CONTACTS AND FIND YOUR RESILIENT COMMUNITY

One of the most important aspects of successful homeschooling is to have or build a strong community of parents, children, and other like-minded people, local to you. If you're friendly with your children's teachers or ex-teachers and they empathize with your choices, they may also know of other parents who homeschool whom they could introduce.

Contact kindergartens, especially those who use Steiner or more liberal, natural models for children's learning, and ask if they know of any existing homeschoolers. Even parents who have homeschooled and whose children are now adults are likely to be good contacts to get to know. There is no substitute for experience, as the saying goes!

Most homeschooling parents will be keen to help others, as they were at the beginning themselves in the past, and are likely to empathize with your new challenges. Never be afraid to ask for help if you feel there's someone in your locality who may be able to assist.

Homeschooling can be interpreted in many different forms, so remember, it isn't necessary to ensure the new homeschooling friends you make are of the same mindset as you are or may become, as you evolve the curriculum that works best for your child. Parents in your community will develop in ways that work for their children too.

In these times of the Coronavirus crisis, many homeschool parents have encouraged their children to study online, but may come to find that a more hands-on, practical approach, or even doing activities and studies together with other children, works far better.

As part of this book, at the end we warmly invite you to become a member of the How and Why community. We want to continue to inform and support you, as community continues to grow. We have other exciting plans too, which we'll be announcing as they develop.

Local homeschoolers, as your community, will become friends. Some, or even yourself, may be single parents who need to work part time and will be glad to meet others with whom you can establish relationships of trust, and thereby leave your children with each other's families by arrangement when needed.

Your local homeschooling community is likely to grow faster now than ever before and continue to multiply as more and more parents and children choose to take schooling into their own hands, where Coronavirus crisis schooling doesn't work for the children.

You and your children will make new friends and thereby avoid isolation, which is key to free homeschooling success. Local homeschool parents with some experience under their belts may also be a helpful and supportive resource for understanding regulations, and can help reduce worries and anxieties, as they welcome new homeschoolers to the local community.

Last and not least, as part of our commitment to homeschoolers globally, now that the book is finished, our intention is to host a weekly podcast, and soon, videos and webinars to help homeschoolers, about which we will be informing you.

3. EXPLORE PREFERRED HOMESCHOOLING METHODS WITH YOUR CHILD

With free homeschooling, your son or daughter is now able to learn as they're most inspired, once they've had sufficient time to unschool themselves.

Remember, on occasion, you may find yourself trying to teach in the same ways as you were taught. When you do, you will quite probably find yourself frustrated with the lack of progress, and your child may often become upset if you insist. If you see such, stop and rethink.

Remember to allow your son the leeway to find the things he is inspired to learn. Your task as a teacher is not to make him wrong, but to observe what he is inspired by, and research what materials (including books) he'll find interesting and what facilities may enable him to progress his learning.

The benefit is in having or creating the facilities at home, or through your local homeschooling community, that are not possible to find in an institutional setting. Watch how your child learns naturally. The free homeschooling environment is not supposed to be a mere replacement to the equivalent of school. To fully benefit from the joys of free homeschooling, you must give your daughter the freedom to let go of the school culture she may have grown used to.

Explore the VARK® Learning Styles, discuss and explore what VARK is, then encourage your daughter to take the downloadable test, which she may find interesting. In this way, you'll both get an understanding of her preferred learning style (there's a good chance you'll get a confirmation of what you've both already observed).

Take a look at Plutchik's Wheel of Emotions, explore and discuss it with your son if he's interested, but do familiarize yourself with it, as coming to understand and be able to recall its makeup may help you on occasion.

Begin to explore free homeschooling with your child and, most importantly, together make sure what you are doing is fun! This is key in learning. Don't forget that children can learn incredibly fast through natural play.

4. TAKE TIME TO EXPLORE THE BEST LEARNING RESOURCES

Only after working through the three prior steps would we recommend moving on to this stage.

There are several ways to free homeschool. In the sub-chapter Homeschool Resources, you'll find carefully researched internet links direct to websites and pages, which will help lead you to begin exploring the different methods that may be of greatest appeal for your child, and which you may also feel most comfortable with.

Try to get free samples first and avoid buying a curriculum too early, which you may later find doesn't work as well as others you'll later discover, which may be a lot more interesting for your child. The Khan Academy, for example, may be too much like normal schooling for your child.

As you meet more people in your local community, it is likely you'll learn from other parents and their children of learning resources they find particularly interesting. They too will probably reinforce the importance of watching what your child's eyes are lit up by, which will encourage you to seek to observe what your child's passions are, and in turn facilitate progress in their chosen direction.

Whether you and your child choose radical free unschooling as a lifestyle of naturally progressive learning to simply set your child free to let his passions lead him, or together you choose a curriculum, or part of one from the resources, we would strongly encourage you to consciously observe your own reactions and let go of how you were taught at school, and know that a set curriculum is not a must have.

Consider it is possible to hinder your child's learning, and even damage their inspirational instincts through forcing him to do what he isn't inspired to.[58]

Explore online and printed homeschool magazines and you'll begin to find more resources that particularly resonate with your child and yourself.

You'll also find in our Bonus Online Chapter – Support the continuously updated Great Homeschool Reading List, which suggests some great books your child may find especially interesting. We'd encourage you to explore the list and purchase books that you feel may be of strong interest. We've started our list from scratch, so if you have any particular book(s) you'd like to submit as special recommendation(s), we'd be thrilled to receive your reviews and recommendations.

5. ATTEND EVENTS, MEETINGS, GATHERINGS, AND BOOK FAIRS

Attending a larger homeschool event can be a great way to meet new people. Many such events will give you a name badge. It may be a good idea to write in smaller letters beneath the region you're from, so others who live not far away may more easily find you.

At such homeschool conventions, you are likely to meet experienced homeschoolers and parents, and the sheer volume of homeschooling resources can be great, if not overwhelming. Not least, it's very possible you and your child will make new friends at these events.

Do look into the ethos of the organization sponsoring the event before attending, as not all may fit with your and your child's perspective, but if you have an open mind, most are worth exploring. For example, when we started researching homeschooling ourselves, when Arina was just a toddler, we attended a quite evangelical organization's event.

That occasion helped us to decide we'd prefer a less religious approach to learning for our children, but we also learned a lot that day. For example, one of the things we learned was just how beneficial reading books can be for children. This came from a great educator who shared how his own education had come largely through reading every book in his local library!

6. SHARE WITH FAMILY AND FRIENDS THAT YOU ARE HOMESCHOOLING

Including the important people in your lives can enable your family to have a better chance at success. Some parents will feel anxious at first about what others may think of unschooling. We ourselves faced this with our direct family and even our neighbors, but after exploring the possibilities, we felt strong conviction in our children's choices and committed our full support. In doing so, what others thought thereafter became much less important.

Years later, we now look back and having shared our progress with family and friends, there are few who don't envy the lifestyle our children have and marvel at the amazing progress that they continue to take strides with.

Grandparents are often a great homeschooling help, since many are retired and often have little else they're more passionately interested in than spending time with family. They have much experience of life and can help our children absorb wisdom, manners and skills they may otherwise not have the chance to. Not least, children build relationships with them, time spent, which they can come to value greatly, as they become grown-ups.

Encourage your children to stay in touch with their friends from kindergarten and school. Especially in the times of the Coronavirus crisis, many children are suffering from the erosion of friendships. It is possible, as they observe the progress of yours, they too may be inspired to explore the idea within their own families.

In turn, if you have made friends with other children's parents from school, we'd encourage you to stay in touch and continue to share how homeschooling has changed life and progress for your child, as progress unfolds.

7. NEVER STOP EXPLORING

Free homeschooling is the freedom to learn, it is not state school. The limits are where we place them, but if we can give our children free rein, they'll keep exploring to continually make new discoveries of their own. To help encourage them to explore, keep expanding the width of their realm of possibility. Take them to museums which house things they're interested in, and give them the freedom to explore.

Travel broadens the mind. Send the kids to places far from home, where they're challenged to return; for example, consider letting your son go hiking and camping within an organized group of friends, once you feel he's mature enough. If you feel he and others may find themselves in trouble, perhaps one or two enthusiastic/experienced parents can join, being mindful to be of minimal interference. Continue to explore ways of learning. If one method doesn't work, say for developing reading, or mathematics, try another more inspiring one, or wait if you sense your timing isn't right. Remember our young children think differently from us adults. They need time to experience, observe, feel, and build the way their minds think. Force isn't effective.

Ask your daughter about what she enjoys and help her continue to expand on this. Where she is attracted to one activity, encourage development and progress along those lines, but also continue to suggest other related or similar activities, or revisit others she wasn't interested in before. Day by day she'll continue learning with joy.

Continue to read books to your son as he grows up. Everybody loves stories. At different times of our lives, different books will appeal. Arina has recently taken an interest in romance novels. That is where her interest is at this point, so we read beautiful love stories to her, which resonate with the values we hold dear.

Through being the best examples we can as parents, we see her developing a good sense of what love is. We trust that when she finds her own future, she'll come to understand what's right for her.

Above all, we parents should ensure that whatever they're learning is fun. When it is so, they lose track of time as they're learning.

15 The Eight Secrets of Homeschooled Geniuses

1. THE POWER IN RELATIONSHIPS

When scientists began studying the health and lives of 268 Harvard sophomores in 1938 during the Great Depression, they hoped the study would show: *What leads to a happy life?*[259]

Over 80 years later, the study continues. Over this time, they studied the adult lives of individuals from the poorest parts of

Boston, to those of the wealthiest families throughout the U.S.A.

Of the original Harvard recruits of 1938, only 19 are still alive, in their mid-90s today. President John F. Kennedy was one of the 1938. (Women weren't in the original study, since at the time, the college only accepted males.)

During the longest study of this type ever conducted, Harvard scientists questioned and interviewed each participant on a bi-annual basis and tracked their happiness. During subsequent decades, the control groups continued to grow. In the '70s, 456 Boston inner-city residents were enlisted, and 40 of them remain alive today. More than a decade ago, researchers began including wives too. "About time," some exclaimed, quite rightly.

The study showed that some went from starting out poor to becoming financially rich, whilst others started rich and some ended up destitute and poor. Some became alcoholics, but there was no inevitable result. Happiness didn't follow the curve of rising, steady or dropping financial wealth. As most of us already knew, money doesn't buy happiness.

Over these years, Harvard researchers studied the participants' health alongside their broader lives, including their failures and successes during their careers and marriages.

"The surprising discovery is that how happy we are in our relationships has a powerful influence on our health," says Robert Waldinger, director of the study and professor of psychiatry at Harvard Medical School. *"Taking care of your body is important, but tending to your relationships is a form of self-care too. This, I think, is the revelation."*

Close relationships are what keep us happy, which in turn strengthen our health. Great relationships keep up our mental stimulation and also delay physical decline. Strong relationships are better predictors of long and happy lives than social class, IQ, or even genes.

Waldinger found that, *"The people who were the most satisfied in their relationships at age 50 we later found were the healthiest at age 80."*

"Those who kept warm relationships got to live longer and happier," said Waldinger, *"and the loners often died earlier."*

"Loneliness kills," he said. *"It's as powerful as smoking or alcoholism."*

Asked what lessons he has learned from the study, Waldinger, who is also a Zen priest, said he practices meditation daily, and actively invests time and energy in relationships around his life, more than before.

Isn't this an amazing finding? Waldinger has said that even being in a toxic relationship of being unhappy or even abused can physically poison our bodies, so they begin to deteriorate sooner.

As parents, it is our responsibility to demonstrate to our children what a warm relationship is, so they in turn will be able to benefit from creating them in their lives. I would venture to say that the ability of our children to create successful, happy relationships in their lives may be of the greatest importance of all.

"Success is not the key to happiness. Happiness is the key to success. If you love what you are doing, you will be successful."

- HERMAN CAIN

"Happiness is not in the mere possession of money; it lies in the joy of achievement, in the thrill of creative effort."

- FRANKLIN D. ROOSEVELT

As I have shared already within this book, to me, relationships are the key to all wealth in our lives, and we are especially empowered when we are selflessly making a difference for others.

If our children's integral way of being is borne of an understanding that **real wealth is what is in our hearts, and it is from that wealth that we go on to create life success,** I believe they will thereby already hold the biggest key to the success of their lives in their hands.

If we, as parents, understand and live by this, the children cannot help but be inspired to live as we do.

2. UNSTOPPABILITY IN SELF-BELIEF.

We have seen the examples of homeschoolers such as Soichiro Honda, founder of Honda Motor Company, and also in Thomas Edison's successes. What is apparent in the amazing life achievements of each of these men, and most other highly successful people that have been homeschooled, is the unflinching self-belief that strengthened them and accompanied their lifetime's successes.

As two inventors and engineers, they were of course faced with countless failures throughout their lives, but they were inexorable in the relentless pursuit of their chosen goals. When they were young, their parents allowed, even encouraged, their children to chase their dreams and somehow both these men learned along the way their inventions or engineering projects just "didn't work," until they'd find the right solution. Inventions and machines don't judge a learner as a teacher might.

Neither Thomas nor Soichiro believed they would ultimately be unable to succeed. They each continued to try and try, till they found solutions to their challenges.

Some of us increasingly see schools as places where, if children are unfortunate enough to not be believed in by their teachers, they may never get to realize the true potential that exists within themselves.[60]

Many schoolchildren grow up to believe they aren't good enough, before they've even attempted to succeed in something they weren't sure they could succeed in. Many schoolchildren learn from an early age to be afraid of failure.

We can see by the examples they were, as people who faced many failures along the way, that neither Soichiro nor Thomas were stopped by mere failure. They saw failure as the integral part of the journey in discovering mistakes and thereby progressing toward success.

If we, as parents that love our children more than anybody else don't believe in them, then who will? We must love, encourage, and acknowledge our children generously, so they grow up believing they can fulfill their dreams. If we do, by the time they grow up, they will already be halfway to the life path they're on the way to finding. But we must have faith in them.

"Whether you believe you can do it, or whether you believe you can't, either way you're absolutely right."

— HENRY FORD

Self-belief is naturally absorbed and developed when children are encouraged to develop naturally. If we observe children, while remembering Jean Piaget's theory of cognitive development, we can see it is the natural process in which a child evolves, given the freedom, environment, stimulation, and materials to explore.

"Play is the shortest route between children and their creative calling."

— VINCE GOWMAN

Encouraging and planting seeds for development through curiosity is a vital part of discovery. The depth of knowledge absorbed is the bedrock of self-belief. When passion makes children forget time while they learn, they in time can discover what they truly love. As they continue to progress and focus on their passion, they develop into their true calling in life.

"Anything that you learn becomes your wealth, a wealth that cannot be taken away from you; whether you learn it in a building called school or in the school of life. To learn something new is a timeless pleasure and a valuable treasure. And not all things that you learn are taught to you, but many things that you learn you realize you have taught yourself."

— C. JOYBELL

Our task as parents is to be there for them.

Your daughter may forge ahead excitedly when you are exploring a mountain together, but stops to look back and make sure you are also there. When your son comes to you to excitedly share his latest project, he does so because he loves to see your eyes share in his excitement.

"Create a set of great personal values and surround yourself with the right people that form your support system. Have an optimistic spirit and develop a strong purpose that you completely believe in and everything you can imagine is possible for you."

- ANDREW HORTON (MOTIVATIONAL SPEAKER)

"You never fail, until you stop trying."

- ALBERT EINSTEIN

3. THE WISDOM OF NATURE

Nature is God's art in motion. It is four-dimensional, where that fourth dimension we can each understand and observe is in the changes that blossom through time.

When we walk in nature, even in the company of others, some of us most enjoy the experience in silence, where we can hear the calling of the wild in the song of birds, small animals, and the streams our paths may cross. Nature, if we observe closely, is of such perfect design that it never wastes of itself.

Everything nature produces benefits something. Weeds heal the soil and stop it being eroded by water and wind and, in turn, weeds die in winter, to feed insects and the soil. Trees living together share nutrients and help one another grow, and even share oxygen through mycelium interconnecting between the roots of neighboring trees.

Peter Wohlleben, author of *The Hidden Life of Trees*[61] writes: *"There are more life forms in a handful of forest soil than there are people on the planet. A mere teaspoonful contains many miles of fungal filaments. All these work the soil, transform it, and make it so valuable for the trees."*

When our children begin to appreciate the beauty of the natural systems that surround us, their curiosity deepens, and they begin to wonder and discover the beauty in her designs. We can also discover with them and together enjoy the wisdom that nature divulges if we explore her ways.

The design and engineering within nature is very much more intelligent than we are. Through all of eternity, humanity is still only just beginning to understand nature. She is here to support our existence, yet man persists in destroying her in the pursuit of personal greed and other short-term gains, while humanity slowly gets ever closer to extinguishing itself. Our children will live well beyond us, we hope, and it is important they embrace and seek to work in harmony, not against nature.

"An organism that is too greedy and takes too much without giving anything in return destroys what it needs for life."

- PETER WOHLLEBEN

Where children learn how nature works, they most naturally learn about life itself. The birth of a small creature may lead to the wonder, curiosity, and ultimately the understanding that their own birth was a beautiful process of nature. Each of us started life from just two tiny cells, one from each of our parents combining!

In the peace and fresh air that nature offers, children can lie in the forest and take time to wonder, imagine, observe and then contemplate, to discover more questions entering their minds than they arrived with that day.

Contemplation is to pierce illusion and experience reality.

Nature offers our children natural wisdom if they listen to her—so give your child every opportunity to be immersed in nature. Create places for her to lie in comfort and look up at the branches of trees swaying in the wind. Take your son to beautiful natural places and let the serenity of God's art enter his mind through what he sees, and in turn, he will begin to love nature, wonder and discover what she offers, and hopefully respect, love and want to live in harmony with nature during his life, and pass what he learns on to his future generations.

"The most beautiful gift of nature is that it gives one pleasure to look around and try to comprehend what we see."

- ALBERT EINSTEIN

4. EXERCISE EQUALS ENDORPHINS. ENDORPHINS MAKE US HAPPY.

Tony Robbins, the world-famous life coach who has improved the lives of millions of people, including some of the world's wealthiest and most successful business leaders, tells us that:[62]

CELLS need to survive and prosper
OXYGEN is the source of all energy
WATER is the most abundant substance in the body
WASTE needs to be eliminated from our cells

He also tells us that if a person does something uninterrupted for 21 or more days, it becomes a natural habit.

Health is one of our primary sources of wealth, yet so many of us ignore its importance, especially the youngest. As we get older, most of the health problems many of us face stem from poor diet, and may be triggered by stress and personal unhappiness. Poor health exacerbates such problems. Obesity in young people has become a (pun intended) growing problem.

Many young homeschoolers take the initiative and love to be outdoors, but not all will do anaerobic activities regularly without some encouragement. As parents, we can help them find active pursuits they enjoy. The key to success is in their enjoyment of activities.

Children who learn to swim well at a young age become great swimmers for life; swimming is said to be the best exercise of all. Cold water is a great way to wake up the body and reinvigorate us. Winter snow sports are activities children and adults can enjoy together if you have such facilities within reach.

When energetic activities become a habit, children don't consider them to be exercise. They're much more exciting! Sailing or windsurfing at a nearby club can help encourage not just an understanding of physics, but spark imagination. For example, how to go faster, or further. It can plant the seed for exploration of the earth by sea, which is a wonderful way to enjoy discovery and adventure together with others as an adult.

Children love to chase one another, or race given the chance. If they learn to skateboard, they challenge themselves to learn new tricks.

Maintaining and maximizing health should become a natural part of everybody's lives, instilled as a lifetime habit. Anaerobic exercise doesn't just help build bodily health, but also helps build self-confidence, discipline, and commitment to what we are focused on.

Martial arts are another great form of exercise, which also help build discipline and commitment, but also help children to learn how to defend themselves should the need ever arise. Dance is a wonderfully fun way to maintain posture and health, so always encourage them to "dance like nobody's watching."

Never stop planting seeds of possibility. Children who naturally exercise while having fun are more likely to develop lifelong habits that will keep them focused in the goals they set themselves.

5. TO PLAY IS TO LEARN

Children are born with more natural learning ability than many of us as parents give them credit for. The very process of play is how children learn fastest. The brain is usually more active during play than it is during study. Play involves focus, concentration, memory power, and logical thinking. As our children play with toys, arts, crafts, and participate in role-play, their imagination, creativity and divergent thinking are stimulated. Play thus ensures wholesome cognitive development.[63]

"Play is the highest form of research."

- ALBERT EINSTEIN

"I never did a day's work in my life. It was all fun."

- THOMAS EDISON

"Anyone who stops learning is old, whether at twenty or eighty. Anyone who keeps learning stays young."

- HENRY FORD

6. DIVERSITY OPENS THE MIND

Diversity in the things that stimulate the minds of children brings with it a variety of wealth of knowledge, experience, and different perspectives. Those differences can be invaluable in their effectiveness of coping with life, developing relationships with others and embracing the differences in others from themselves, innovation, problem solving, insight, creativity, and more.

Although during the Coronavirus crisis many of us have been

unable to travel abroad, hopefully in the not too distant future, restrictions may be lifted. When they are, aim to give your children the opportunity to explore if you are able to.[64]

Traveling as a family when young, then alone when they're more grown up and responsible, is a great way for children not only to learn new things, but to immerse themselves in a new culture. Travel can provide irresistible stimulation for the continued enjoyment of learning, as children discover places, cultures, and the different ways of living they may never otherwise have realized existed.

"The real voyage of discovery is not in seeking new landscapes but in having new eyes."

– MARCEL PROUST

When children travel abroad, they may get to prove to themselves just how capable they are, such as beginning to learn to speak and express themselves in a new language. When these endeavors are successful, **they can thereby discover a newfound confidence that holds them in good stead for the future.**

The world is like a book and those who do not travel read only one page.

7. MUSIC ENHANCES MENTAL DEVELOPMENT

All highly intelligent people are not necessarily musical, but would it be fair to say that highly musical people are highly intelligent? Let's leave this thought till later, after we examine how playing a musical instrument may positively impact a child's learning:

Music appeals to the sense of hearing, which is one of the four ways the VARK® model shows we absorb information and learn. During such learning processes, connections are made between neurons of our brain. Music helps to develop the left of the brain (the analytical and methodical side).

When live performing, say with sheet music, the memory is

being simultaneously accessed, as the eyes read and the hands or other parts of the body are coordinated in fine movements to, say, press the keys on a piano. Learning music successfully is achieved through passion and a commitment to achieving a quality of body movements to produce the targeted musical result.

Listening to music also helps the development of a more acute sense of sound and distinction between instruments, as sensory perception broadens through experiences.

Playing music is normally rewarding for the musician, paid in a sense of satisfaction.

Further pattern-recognition skills are naturally developed through music, which are said to be similar in logic to some mathematical procedures. **Imagination and intellectual curiosity are aroused when making music too, and through repetition, in pursuit of perfecting the learning of said musical instrument, children can experience a development of self-discipline.**

Music can invoke very strong emotional response too, which may cement particular events as more poignant memories than a given event might otherwise have been had there not been music.

For some, performing in public can bring fear and anxiety, and just as with public speaking, the action of doing so regardless may show your daughter that to face one's fears she comes to realize that what she'd feared, in reality, isn't as scary as she may have imagined.

"Intelligence" comes from the Latin word "*intelegere*," which is the verb to understand. The question remains whether or not music does improve homeschooled children's intelligence?

Most would agree, accomplished musicians undoubtedly have a finer and more developed sense of musical tone. It may be fair to surmise thereby, if your daughter can understand sounds better, then her intelligence by definition is on a higher level than if she hadn't learned to play a musical instrument.

Similarly, as we know, learning two languages as a child builds many more connections in the brain than otherwise. Learning two languages has been shown to help improve problem-solving abilities, or even the imagination. Studying music, similarly, leads to building more neuron links within the brain.[65]

The amount of improvement of intelligence would be impossible to quantify, but if we look at the next category, which most of us would agree is true, then we might look back and agree music most certainly does positively impact the brain's development.

Lastly, I'd like to end this category with this beautiful quotation:

"If art is how we decorate space, music is how we decorate time."

- JEAN MICHEL BASQUIAT

8. READING EVOLVES INTELLIGENCE

The last category, at the risk of repeating what has already been said elsewhere in this book, is one of the most important that I feel has made a personal and profound difference to me, and the lives of some of my closest friends.

Indeed, what they have learned from reading and sometimes shared during fascinating conversations has in turn impacted my thinking on occasion.

Reading can greatly stimulate the imagination and invoke every possible emotion. Reading improves knowledge, expands the vocabulary, and thereby helps strengthen your child's confidence. Although what a child can experience from reading a story is not a personal experience, it can be valid enough that a child understands what the response would have been in a narrated scenario.

Books can help develop a child's emotional intelligence because a story elicits real emotional responses in the reader. From crying to laughter, to joy, to anger—reading can stimulate a wide array of emotions, giving the reader an opportunity to recognize these feelings and better regulate their own during real-world situations.

Reading can improve social perception and even increase the sense of empathy. As we know, books also encourage contemplation, which is to access the imagination.

"Imagination is more important than knowledge. Knowledge is limited. Imagination encircles the world."

– ALBERT EINSTEIN

Scientists don't yet fully understand how the imagination works, or even in which parts of the brain (or even the realm of dreaming in our sleep) imaginative processes work, but we can be certain it is through the processes that occur through connections of millions of neurons.[66]

If there's one thing we should never give up on, but always gently encourage, it is the reading of books beyond the day it ignites a passion for books within our children. It can take longer for some children than others, but if you believe in your children's greatness, they're that one step closer to believing in themselves.

Every child loves to hear a great story, and in time, they come to love reading them for themselves.

16 How Do Homeschool Kids End Up In Life?

If we take just a little time to search, we find there are many people who we recognize as celebrities, both in the past and present, who were homeschooled.

Within just 20 years, three individuals who were homeschooled served as U.S. presidents: George Washington was the first president of the United States, Thomas Jefferson the third president of the United States, and James Madison the fourth president.

Franklin D. Roosevelt, the 32nd President. Abraham Lincoln

finished one year of formal schooling. He taught himself trigonometry, and went on to become a lawyer before going on to being elected U.S. president.

Condoleezza Rice, diplomat, political scientist, civil servant, and professor who is the current director of the Hoover Institution at Stanford University, U.S. national security advisor between 2001-2005, was homeschooled.

Wolfgang Amadeus Mozart was homeschooled. By the age of five, he was composing and performing before royalty. Mozart went on to compose more than 600 works before his untimely death when aged just 35.

Alexander Graham Bell, inventor, was homeschooled by his mother, just as Thomas Edison was.

Thomas' mother had been a schoolteacher, but it is interesting she didn't feel it necessary to force Thomas to attend school. She knew he was smart and gave him room to develop himself.

Lewis Carroll was a mathematician and authored *Alice in Wonderland*.

Virginia Woolf was a celebrated novelist and so many other famous authors that most of us will recognize were homeschooled, ranging from Jane Austen, Hans Christian Andersen, Beatrix Potter, Agatha Christie, Charles Dickens, C.S Lewis, to Mark Twain.

Great scientists and thinkers, such as Leonardo Da Vinci, Albert Einstein and Isaac Newton learned at home, while pursuing their interests and passions.

Two brothers, Orville and Wilbur Wright, using knowledge developed through play became the very first to fly successfully using a gasoline engine.

Of course, almost 300 years was a long time ago when the first presidents of the United States were elected. Back then, little existed in the way of public schooling, but is the above list of famous names we all know not ample evidence that attending school is not as essential as some believe?

More recently, in 1988, David and Micki Colfax published *Homeschooling for Excellence; How to take charge of your child's education, and why you absolutely must.*

Without electricity, running water, or even a phone, they

homeschooled their four boys, three of whom were adopted. Although they didn't start out with the intention of their sons attending Harvard, that's what they went on to achieve— three with full scholarships!

Their family's homeschooling was simple: It focused on encouraging and facilitating a natural love for learning, drawing on facilities to allow the children to develop their unique talents, at their own pace. Some of their children didn't even learn to read until they were seven or eight years old. Still, they didn't find anything wrong, nor did they shuffle them off to all kinds of academic lessons.

Their boys spent much of their early years outdoors on their farm, working in creative ways. Their boys each enjoyed drawing knowledge from their incredibly large home library.

Today, their son Grant Colfax is the Director of the Office of National AIDS Policy. The president's lead advisor on domestic HIV/AIDS, he is responsible for overseeing implementation of the National HIV/AIDS strategy, and guiding HIV/AIDS policies across federal agencies.

David Karp is the founder of the microblogging and social networking site Tumblr. At 15, he dropped out of his Bronx high school and used his time in intensive exploration of the computer world, which was his primary passion. Just a few years after, he started his professional career, which led him to where he is today, now in his 30s.

Many household names even our children know, including Whoopi Goldberg, the Jonas Brothers, Serena and Venus Williams, Ryan Gosling, Justin Timberlake, Justin Bieber, Emma Watson, Demi Lovato and Selina Gomez each spent time in their childhoods in varying degrees being homeschooled. These people are advocates of the benefits of homeschooling.

I could go on listing other heroes of homeschooling, or writing of the famous parents who are currently homeschooling their children. Yet again, no doubt a fascinating book could be written of their stories, triumphs, and achievements, but I'm sure you get the picture.

Some may argue that many more state-schooled children went on to become great achievers in their lives, and of course they'd be right. This chapter is not intended as a comparison. I have listed the individuals above to give some idea, and there are many I haven't mentioned here.

Of course, just as for state-schooled individuals, there are many homeschooled individuals we will never know of who have gone on to do great things in their lives. Many have chosen to reintegrate with society and live normal lives, working in normal careers, or bringing up their own families.

Of the people I have known for decades, some went on to become teachers, some are businesspeople, others became artists, builders, entertainers, musicians, and some became scholars. One became a well-known international model who has since quit the catwalk to pursue a career in knitwear and fashion design. Many have traveled and settled in different countries.

There is no predicting where our homeschooled children may end up in life...

What we see of those homeschooled kids we have watched grow into young adults is that they are happy, and several of them have become experts in the passions they fostered as children. Passions in which, in many cases, their parents played little or no part in fostering. Their parents simply provided facilities and materials to make possible their reality.

We believe that development of a child's abilities and knowledge borne of a passion for discovery is far more empowering to the individual than through a typically academic system of memorization, repetition, and testing.

Ultimately, if we parents don't have faith in our children, then who else will?

We seek to encourage our children through the path of developing their hobbies and interests, which in turn is likely to self-drive their desire to know more and stands to ultimately lead them to the path of their calling. Along the way, they'll find the need to learn sciences, languages, mathematics, philosophy, and much more.

In this way, children stand a better chance of becoming confident, driven and inspiring individuals, who may someday become leaders in their chosen careers.

Comparing the above to the alternative of being coerced to learn so they become good at passing exams, then push them into vocations that may ultimately help them gain financial wealth, with far less likelihood they'll actually have a passion for what they end up doing, is a choice some parents may find some discomfort in contemplating, but it's a spiral many children sadly find themselves in.

These children, in many cases, may grow up to become people who in future, should they stop to look deeply, realize their career choices may have been made through a deeply seated fear of failure, which may be imbued through pressures from teachers, parents, family, and friends, most of whom may never have looked deeply at the true costs of being afraid to fail.

Fear of failure is debilitating, and rarely engenders true greatness in a person's life. It can and often is skillfully hidden. It would be fair to observe that a fear of failure can lead to financial success, often visible through material wealth, but if fear of failure is the primary driver in the choices we make then we might ask ourselves if this is something we want to pass on to the children we love as the true meaning of success.[67]

Is a life led by fear of failure how we *really* want to inspire our children to make progress?

Yuko and I know family members, friends and acquaintances on both sides of the fence. We've known many successful professionals from the time they were young students work their way over decades to reach the top of their field of expertise. Corporate lawyers, multinational CEOs, surgeons, doctors, dentists, finance professionals, pharmaceutical marketing managers, etc.

I look back and can say without doubt most "successful professionals" I know have no passion for their work.

A minority of those I have known much of my life who are able to save lots of money working in jobs they find stressful and often unpleasant either have, or are likely to eventually quit, when they realize they have never done the things they're far more interested in pursuing, and realize they're running out of time.

Some have found themselves delaying till later, and some didn't live to escape the trap. Those tragically lost what time they had, and passed away, sometimes unhappy workaholics, whose greatest triumph in life has been accumulation of material wealth. Some of these people I've known died as very wealthy individuals, but I wouldn't consider them truly successful myself. Throughout my years of knowing them, I rarely saw them be truly happy.

I've observed many such "successful people" sacrifice most of the waking hours of their lives for the comforts money can buy them, and the security that money can someday afford their children. We observed that such individuals often don't have much time for their children and spent little valuable time together with their spouses. Instead, they focused on making more and more money. To what end? Is this really what we mean to become successful?[68]

In our community here in Japan, we know many people on the other side of the fence. From permaculturalists who have little need for money to live, but have total freedom to do what they're inspired to each day, to people who run niche businesses and can make a decent living in doing what they love.

I include myself in this latter category: I faced my fears of failure in the early years of my career and made choices which have led me on a continuously wondrous path of life together with my family.

Twenty-three years ago, I chose not to be controlled by my deeply instilled fear of failure when I realized how my life would never have a chance to progress if I didn't give up being controlled by fear. Today I can honestly look back with no regrets. Instead, I am relieved I was able to make choices from the heart, and enjoy the great adventures that have and continue to ensue.

For me, some of my most valuable learning was borne from having been given the freedom to play and learn through passion when I learned skills with my father, as a young boy, during my own experiences of free homeschooling.

The freedoms I allowed myself while attending university and thereafter to travel widely, experience and build relationships, ultimately led me to the life I have enjoyed in Japan since 1998. I enjoy a continued freedom together with our family today and it is without doubt the life I would choose were I to go back and could make choices again.

Yuko feels much the same. She strengthens me in her resolve, support, and love for who I am as a person. I naturally reciprocate love, honoring her for the great lady she is.

These are the values and wisdoms Yuko and I want to pass on to our children. We all spend time together daily and instill ways in which they'll learn to create income; making money to sustain their lives is a game that is to be enjoyed while building great relations with others. The ability to create a comfortable, sustainable, healthy life is something we shouldn't be afraid of failure at. Failure is a stepping-stone of the path to success.

I tell our kids we want to share all that we know with them, so they can take what serves them to create the lives they in turn are inspired to live.

So don't be afraid, dear parent. Hunt out fears of failure and be mindful of how debilitating they can be for each of our lives. Encourage your children to make better and more empowering choices that stem from a zest for life and their freedom to explore.

17 The Future of Homeschooling

Between March 2020 and March 2021, the education sector changed in unprecedented ways that none of us would ever have predicted. Due to the pandemic, some schools closed entirely, initially for a couple of weeks, months, then in some cases, for almost the entire year.

Hundreds of millions of children throughout the world were suddenly displaced from their classrooms and told they must learn at home, as part of the Covid-19 response. At its peak, that number reached an estimated 1.5 billion children.[69]

Some schools did their best to adapt and resorted to the development of remote learning in an effort for children to finish what was left of the school year. The rate of success in online schooling was so low that in the U.K. (where public schools were generally open longer during the year than in the U.S.) examinations normally used for university entrance were cancelled, and instead, children were graded according to how their teacher rated the quality of their work throughout the Coronavirus crisis year.[70]

Where schools were reopened, some children have been required to socially distance, spray their hands with alcohol, wear masks, have their temperatures takes on arrival and, in some cases, required to wear face shields. Most recently as I write, we have seen governments of First World countries around the world roll out vaccines for 12-15-year-old school attendees, regardless of the fact that the U.K.'s vaccine advisory body refused to recommend vaccinating them.[71]

As I write, even after experimental mRNA vaccines have been introduced and approved widely within the previously unprecedented space of just a year, there is no sign these measures are to be dropped. Instead, mainstream news and government (U.K. NHS) directives now inform us that these mRNA vaccines lose their efficacy, and we should have top-up jabs for our own protection.[72]

We have learned being vaccinated doesn't mean children cannot transmit, or even avoid catching the latest Coronavirus. Measures to return normality do not appear to be returning for the majority of children. More masks, social distancing, and now jabs for kids are on the cards.[73]

When much of the world first went into lockdowns from March 2020, many assumed that the pandemic might lead to a baby boom. The opposite turned out. We're suffering an alarming Coronavirus baby bust, with birth rates in European countries falling by 20% or more, to levels not seen since the Second World War.[74]

As early as June last year, researchers at the Brookings Institution in Washington were warning of a baby bust. Contrary to the *"persistent myths about birth spikes occurring nine months after blizzards or major electricity blackouts… the Covid-19 crisis is amounting to much more than a temporary stay-at-home order. It is leading to tremendous economic loss, uncertainty, and insecurity. That is why birth rates will tumble."*

Uncertainties of the future with worries about housing, employment and income, as well as people being unable to socialize or see one another's faces, have all contributed to fewer people starting new relationships, getting married, and many are postponing having children. Many weddings were also postponed due to lockdown restrictions.

Children, whose innocent lives have been drastically affected, are facing a future at school that, as we continue seeing measures continue to be expanded worldwide, with the now rolling out of vaccines, likely followed by Covid-19 passports, etc., that is looking ever less positive.[75]

Globally, childhood depression has skyrocketed in the last year, and tragically, so too have childhood (and adult) suicides.[76]

Children have missed a year of vital socializing with their friends and extended family and see little hope of a return to normality. I could go on, but as a concerned parent reading this book, you may already have observed how your child's life has been affected and have probably already felt the need to do something, which is why you may have searched for and read this book.

Homeschooling is clearly not yet as mainstream as regular schools, but it has been growing exponentially. Since the 80s, especially in the U.S., homeschooling has been receiving ever increasing acceptance and is where it is has become most adopted in the world.

A study the U.S. Department of Education published at the beginning of 2017, about parents' involvement in education, showed that parental apprehension about the environment of conventional state schooling was growing, where a main concern was of the quality of education children were being given.[77][78]

Moreover, studies increasingly show that homeschoolers are more likely to achieve a better academic performance. Many have a higher chance of fulfilling high-school graduation requirements and entering college sooner than would be usual.[79]

The atmosphere of most homeschooling can be much more conducive and effective for learning. The love, empathy and guidance of some parents is also incredibly helpful in encouraging a child's concentration.

While the public experienced a health calamity in 2020, the fast-growing homeschooling community realized this was a huge opportunity to expand and share with other concerned parents the benefits that are possible.

In the last year, it's hardly surprising more parents have become untrusting of the government-controlled school environment being healthy for the mental health of their children. The now prevalent issues on Coronavirus crisis issues, added to safety issues, alcohol and drugs, peer pressure, emerging behavioral, emotional, and mental problems that some parents have become concerned about are increasingly making traditional education a daunting prospect, both for kids and parents.[80]

Those of us who had already started homeschooling our kids years prior to the school shutdowns could clearly see that pandemic homeschooling when introduced would not reflect even similar homeschooling style we and many other families have found works.

To be forcibly separated as so many kids were from extended family, friends and local communities, and in many cases not be allowed to visit public places, had very difficult consequences for a great many families who had left their children's education to state schools. We have been unsurprised to find the global interest in homeschooling has grown in record numbers.

Despite this unexpected and inauspicious introduction to online schooling, for millions of parents and students it appeared this was the only feasible option they were offered.

One of the earliest signs that the Coronavirus crisis would lead to a large growth in the homeschooling movement became apparent in April 2020's Edchoice.org survey of parents. The survey enquired how families were coping with school shutdowns.

Within just a month of lockdown measures, more than half of the respondents confirmed they had a more favorable view of homeschooling than they'd had before the pandemic began. Indeed, most parents who said they now considered homeschooling as a viable solution had probably never even considered the option before.[81]

In May 2020, in a https://www.federationforchildren.org survey conducted nationally in the U.S., many parents confirmed they were more satisfied with at-home learning than they'd expected. Even more encouragingly, 40% said they were more likely to continue homeschooling or virtual learning if schools were reopened. Other polls, such as USA Today and Ipsos, reported similar findings.

Many parents have had their professional lives disrupted and subsequently spent more time than ever at home with the children. Staff of many multinational companies report that they had been working from home for most of the 2020 year.

Work-related travel costs were slashed.

Many working parents have relished spending much more time around the kids instead of having to travel daily to their office. The less fortunate parents among us may have had no choice but to redesign careers. Some have become afraid of being around others in a work environment due to health fears.

As summer 2020 began, parents and students reaffirmed poll predictions. Registrations of intent to leave the school system and become independent homeschoolers increased to unprecedented levels in the U.S.[82]

In North Carolina, so many submitted online forms of intent to homeschool that the state's nonpublic education website crashed. In Nebraska, homeschool declarations increased by 21%. In Vermont, declarations of intending homeschoolers increased by a staggering 75% between 2020 and 2021.[83]

Grassroots and small Facebook homeschooling networks also reported record increases in membership.

Not surprisingly, education startups such as getSchoolHouse. com took advantage of the Coronavirus crisis. Other education-related platforms, such as outschool.com offering thousands of live, virtual classes of a large range of subjects, for kids of all ages, saw demand soar and investment has skyrocketed.

Zoom, the video conferencing app, has grown in value by almost three times, according to marketwatch.com as I write. Such developments as these are still only the beginning.

Video conferencing and education tech companies are growing and here to stay. It's only a matter of time before other new tech startups begin to roll out more online solutions. (Naturally, we'd advocate less screen time, to instead encourage more time spent outdoors surrounded by nature.)

School shutdowns throughout the world have inspired many families to take a closer look at their children's education and to consider better homeschooling alternatives. Perhaps they had been curious about homeschooling but lacked the catalyst to give it a try until now. Parents may be noticing their children are learning more outside of a conventional classroom and appreciate greater educational freedom and personalization.

Many U.S. schools are now reporting a drop in enrollment numbers, and thereby state funding.[84] What, pre-pandemic, was already desperately low funding for many schools is expected to continue to decline. Privatization of public education has been developing, and the now apparent decline in funding at a time when it should be increased is becoming increasingly likely to bring the running of facilities into severe financial challenges going forward.

Billionaire Betsy De Vos served as Secretary of Education under U.S. President Donald Trump from 2017 to 2021. Since the beginning of her time in U.S. government, she was a staunch supporter of privatization of public schools in the U.S.[85]

Privatization of public schools in the U.S. has been a planned push by policymakers to shift public education funds and students into the private sector. A voucher system has been used to encourage parents to move toward privately run schools as an attempt to contract with for-profit entities for various responsibilities that have long been the responsibility of the public sector.

To add to the fire, according to some mainstream news sources, some teachers' unions indicated members prefer to delay a return to work, citing fears of the re-emergence of Coronavirus numbers, which in turn may lead to some uncertainty, and yet more long-term disruption.[86]

In response, it would appear there have been developments of schools' online classes. A trend which sadly continues gaining increasing acceptance not just in the U.S. but worldwide.

The world has begun to understand and accept that the longer the effects and lockdowns go on, the less likelihood there will be a return to how things were before. Families are continuing to leave traditional schooling in droves now in 2021, and the trend is likely to continue into 2022 and beyond.

Ripples turn to waves, triggering what started as a relatively small but important educational change. As pre-pandemic normality fails to return, we can expect ripples of interest to turn to larger waves of adoption of homeschooling.

Yuko and I, having seen the difference free homeschooling has made for many children already, can see that early adopters of free homeschooling through passion are the ones who will ultimately benefit most.

We foresee homeschooling will continue to grow as the smartest option for parents who don't want to leave their children's education to a system that has, especially during the Coronavirus crisis, largely failed and is likely to continue to decline, and not recover.

Humanity is embarking on the Fourth Industrial Revolution. It's no longer a matter of "if" jobs will be replaced by AI, but when.[87]

Yuko and I expect that by the time our two children become adults (around 2030), AI will have become the norm and not the exception. We have been preparing them, while giving them the wealth that comes from having the healthiest, most loving and most interesting childhood of natural learning we can give them.

The following was written by a friend's daughter, while observing the effects of Coronavirus shutdowns:

"Although academic learning is important, when we children are together, we learn the importance of communication. Children live to learn. To prepare ourselves for a great future, we cannot simply know about academic subjects, but must develop skills in being with other people: To dream together, make choices and take risks. It is when together with friends and family that we children learn that to cry is as normal as laughing. To have a difference of opinion is not a reason to separate ourselves, it's an opportunity to expand our relationships and continue to learn. It is in building relationships with one another that children appreciate the opportunities to take risks in life is what makes our lives exciting."

If you've already chosen to become homeschoolers, then I'd like to acknowledge your commitment in the face of some of the biggest challenges you may have ever faced. Know that you are not alone. You are part of a growing global movement that produces some of the most talented adults of the future.

"As you sow so shall you reap."

- ANONYMOUS

Those of us who can vividly remember our childhoods three decades ago or a little less might have noticed the slow decline in education standards at state schools, to where things were in 2019, and then during the Coronavirus crisis.

"The quality of your life is the quality of your relationships."

- TONY ROBBINS

Social media has changed the face of our children's relationships with one another over the last decade, at ever more alarming rates. Rates of childhood depression were already higher than ever in 2019, ominously due to a decline in relationship quality and social media.

In 2020, we saw government throughout the world bring a further unprecedented decline in the quality of state schooling. We've observed the continued rollout of online state schooling.[88]

The results are questionable when there are more reports than ever of childhood depression, with few if any attempts to present positive solutions.

Is this the level of education we parents really want for our children? NO!

Those of us who see where education is being steered, and see the dangers of current and future educational developments, must share and be a part of creating the better solution, to make a difference for as many others as we can. Our children deserve better and we will be the example that will lead other families into enquiring why our kids are so happy in their childhoods, and so talented.

In the face of this slow but continued erosion of state schooling, the ingenuity that parents, children and the emerging homeschooling world can make is of a vast positive difference. What we can do for our children will long outlast the pandemic to give them and others in future a more empowering, independent education.

Homeschooling is here. It is a movement of now, where together as a fast-growing courageous global community of homeschoolers we are taking back control of how and what our children learn. We are combining to help one another through joined homeschooling communities of highly skilled, uniquely talented, charismatic thinkers, doers and leaders of tomorrow. Powerful children will awake and inspire others throughout their lives ahead.[89] [90]

We must never lose sight of the vision that is possible, nor believe we are to be controlled, nor to "own nothing and be happy."[91]

We, together with our children, are the brightest future we are inspired to create. We shall make the difference, not just for ourselves and humanity, but the grandchildren and grandchildren's grandchildren of humanity.

Our purpose in free homeschooling is not merely for ourselves, but countless others who all deserve to live in the freedom of who they are most inspired to be.

We, together with our children, are the sparks of love that will spread into a burning quest for knowledge to be shared, generations ahead, with which they'll make the brightest future.

BONUS CHAPTER – SUPPORT

Now that I've shared with you as much as we can up to this point, I don't want to just leave it at that…OH NO!

I'd love to get to know you, and help you as much as I can, so each of our children's futures can be as bright as possible.

We're continuously developing new ideas, techniques and better free homeschool learning methods, discovering more amazing books that will enchant children, great educational tools and materials.

I do hope you'll allow us to share this ever growing wealth of knowledge.

If you haven't already, visit www.howtohomeschool.life and join our mailing list. Once you have given your name and email and password, you'll instantly be given access to:

The Homeschool Genius Reading List

Free Homeschool Podcasts

Free Homeschool Videos

And more, as we produce more exciting developments!

Now I must confess, I'm really not a keen social media contributor, and will quite possibly refrain from becoming one in the foreseeable future… but if you are one, and would be keen to join our homeschool team, we'd love to hear from you!

The vision I am committed to going forward is to build a community of 100,000 like-minded free homeschoolers throughout the world who can come together, contribute to one another, and grow up to become an empowered and large group of unique individuals who are free to live, create and become the empowered adults our children each have an inner calling for.

I am absolutely committed to achieving this, with and for you, by the end of 2023.

Can we do it?

Whether you believe we can, or whether you believe we cannot, either way you're absolutely right—ha!

I look forward to being in community with you.

Stay positive!

Love

Miguel

About the Author

Miguel Varella-Cid has a deep commitment to a healthy family life. He and his wife Yuko believe a strong education, knowledge and skills gained through facilitating development of their greatest interests, immersion in nature, and the natural ability to create great relationships with others, are each of key importance for the development of children.

They have created and gained much recognition in Japan for the unique free homeschooling methods they have developed. Miguel is the founder and presenter of the weekly *Why and How* podcast. He and family regularly present at educational events in Japan, and more recently on NHK Television.

Notes

WHAT MAKES CHILDREN SMART

1   "Thomas Edison, National Historical Park, NJ, U.S.A. Edison Biography,"
https://www.nps.gov/edis/learn/historyculture/edison-biography.htm

2   Henry Ford Quotations,
https://www.thehenryford.org/collections-and-research/digital-resources/popular-topics/henry-ford-quotes/

3   Alfred Mercier, "A Passion for Lifelong Learning: what we learn with pleasure we never forget," https://kaba.org/passion-lifelong-learning/

4   Mark Weston and Katie Yamasaki, *The Story of Car Engineer Soichiro Honda,*
https://www.amazon.com/Soichiro-Honda-Books/s?k=Soichiro+Hondaand rh=n%3A283155

5   Avery Hunt, "How Learning a Language Changes Your Brain,"
https://www.discovermagazine.com/mind/how-learning-a-language-changes-your-brain

6   The University of Queensland, Australia – Queensland Brain Institute: "Does Music Make Us Smarter?"
https://qbi.uq.edu.au/blog/2018/01/does-music-make-us-smarter

7   "Feeling loved in everyday life linked with improved well-being," https://www.sciencedaily.com/releases/2019/11/191125121005.htm

HOW TO HOMESCHOOL

8   Gardiner Morse, *Harvard Business Review,* "Decisions and Desire,"
https://hbr.org/2006/01/decisions-and-desire

9   "The Emotional Wheel. What It Is, and How to Use It" [PDF],
https://positivepsychology.com/emotion-wheel/

FREE HOMESCHOOL CURRICULUM

10   Karen Young, "Building Courage in Kids – How to Teach Kids to be Brave,"
https://www.heysigmund.com/building-courage-in-kids/

11   Neil Burton M.D., "The Psychology of Laziness, Procrastination, and Idleness,"
https://www.psychologytoday.com/us/blog/hide-and-seek/201410/the-psychology-laziness

12   Ralph Ryback M.D., "The Powerful Psychology Behind Cleanliness – The Truism of Wellness,"
https://www.psychologytoday.com/us/blog/the-truisms-wellness/201607/the-powerful-psychology-behind-cleanliness

13   "Respecting Social Norms: Manners and Etiquette Rules Kids Should Know,"
https://superkidz.com/respecting-social-norms/

14   Erik H. Erikson, *Identity and the Life Cycle,*
https://www.goodreads.com/book/show/56013.Identity_and_the_Life_Cycle

15   "The Importance of Socialization,"
https://pressbooks.howardcc.edu/soci101/chapter/4-1-the-importance-of-socialization/

16   The Landmark Forum Website, "Transformative Learning, Offering Life-Changing Awareness and Wisdom," https://www.landmarkworldwide.com

17   Permaculture Australia is a member-based, not-for-profit organization that promotes and advocates for permaculture ideas, solutions and strategies across Australia and the world,
https://permacultureaustralia.org

18   Jeff S., "How Important are Public Speaking Skills for Kids?"
https://takelessons.com/blog/public-speaking-skills

FACING YOUR HOMESCHOOL FEARS

19   Klaus Schwab and Thierry Malleret, "Covid-19: The Great Reset," https://stevenguinness2.wordpress.com/2020/09/03/thoughts-on-covid-19-the-great-reset-by-klaus-schwab-and-thierry-malleret/

HEALTH IS OUR WEALTH

20 "Eating Well for Mental Health,"
https://www.sutterhealth.org/health/nutrition/eating-well-for-mental-health

21 "The Top 10 Plant-Based Milk Alternatives,"
https://huel.com/pages/the-top-10-plant-milk-alternatives

22 "Plant-Based Eating Simplified," Forks Over Knives.com,
https://www.forksoverknives.com/

23 Mary L. Gavin, M.D., "What Sleep Is and Why All Kids Need It,"
https://kidshealth.org/en/kids/not-tired.html

THE MYTHS OF HOMESCHOOLING

24 David McCarthy, "Are online schools the future of Education?" A biased view, promoting the notion for the future of schooling without discussing the detrimental consequences on children,
https://www.openaccessgovernment.org/are-online-schools-the-future-of-education/96076/

25 Proposal for a push for online schooling in Japan (supported already by Rakuten, one of Japan's fastest growing internet and mobile phone service providers), https://www8.cao.go.jp/cstp/english/society5_0/index.html

THE DIGITAL PACIFIER

26 Tristan Harris, "We're 10 years into this mass hypnosis,"
https://www.52-insights.com/interview-social-media-tristan-harris-were-10-years-into-this-mass-hypnosis/

27 Jaron Lanier, *Ten Arguments For Deleting Your Social Media Accounts Right Now*, https://www.goodreads.com/book/show/37830765-ten-arguments-for-deleting-your-social-media-accounts-right-now

28 50 Quotes - Chamath Palihapitiya,
https://wealthygorilla.com/chamath-palihapitiya-quotes/

FREE HOMESCHOOLING, THE CORONAVIRUS CRISIS AND THE GREAT RESET

29   John Hopkins Medicine, "New Variants of Corona Virus: What You Should Know," https://www.hopkinsmedicine.org/health/conditions-and-diseases/coronavirus/a-new-strain-of-coronavirus-what-you-should-know

30   J.D. Rucker, "The White House Warns More Lockdowns Are Coming,"
https://americanconservativemovement.com/2021/07/29/white-house-warns-more-lockdowns-are-coming/

31   Akane Okutsu, Nikkei staff writer, "Tokyo Governor Says Lockdown in Japan is Impossible,"
https://asia.nikkei.com/Editor-s-Picks/Interview/Tokyo-governor-says-lockdown-in-Japan-is-impossible

32   "A Brief History of Mask Wearing in Japan," Nippon.com,
https://www.nippon.com/en/features/jg00084/

33   "Pfizer testing Oral Covid Drug,"
https://www.reuters.com/business/healthcare-pharmaceuticals/pfizer-starts-dosing-patients-oral-covid-19-drug-trial-2021-09-01/

34   Dr. Mike Yeadon, 32 years highly qualified professional experience Allergy and Respiratory Research, and ex vice-president of research at Pfizer – full interview,
https://www.bitchute.com/video/LKkuwLFDPcav/

35   Betsy De Vos – A brief summary of some of the legal battles she was embroiled in as Education Secretary – focusing on diverting public funding to private educational establishments,
https://educationvotes.nea.org/2019/03/22/devos/

36   "Excessive and Problematic Internet Use During the Coronavirus Disease 2019 School Closure,"
https://www.ncbi.nlm.nih.gov/pmc/articles/PMC7773910/

37   "Students are falling behind, and teachers are stressed as schools go online. But there's still no grand plan to improve virtual learning,"
https://www.usatoday.com/in-depth/news/education/2020/12/13/covid-online-school-tutoring-plan/6334907002/

38 **"What Happens When Kids Don't See Their Peers for Months,"**
https://www.theatlantic.com/family/archive/2020/06/how-quarantine-will-affect-kids-social-development/613381/

39 **"Youth suicide attempts soared during pandemic, CDC report says,"**
https://www.nbcnews.com/news/us-news/youth-suicide-attempts-soared-during-pandemic-cdc-report-says-n1270463

40 **"COVID-19 and the Use of Masks by Children,"** https://www.frontiersin.org/articles/10.3389/fped.2021.580150/full

41 **"Social, Political, Economic, and Psychological Consequences of the COVID-19 Pandemic,"**
https://www.russellsage.org/research/funding/covid-19-pandemic

42 **"What Makes a Good Life? Lessons from the Longest Study on Happiness,"**
https://www.ted.com/talks/robert_waldinger_what_makes_a_good_life_lessons_from_the_longest_study_on_happiness?language=en

43 **Larry Elliot,** *The Guardian*, **"The Demise of the Middle Class,"**
https://www.theguardian.com/commentisfree/2019/may/03/demise-middle-classes-british-politics-digital-age

44 **"Conspiracy theories aside, there is something fishy about the Great Reset,"** https://www.opendemocracy.net/en/oureconomy/conspiracy-theories-aside-there-something-fishy-about-great-reset/

45 **Klaus Schwab,** *COVID-19: The Great Reset,*
https://www.amazon.com/COVID-19-Great-Reset-Klaus-Schwab/dp/2940631123

46 **Amazon.com.inc., "Revenue Rose 26% from a Year Earlier Through March 2020,"**
https://www.wsj.com/articles/amazons-sales-jump-as-coronavirus-prompts-surge-in-online-shopping-11588278740

47 **"25 Giant Corporations that are Bigger Than Entire Countries,"** https://www.businessinsider.com/25-giant-companies-that-earn-more-than-entire-countries-2018-7

48 **G Edward Griffin,** *The Creature from Jekyll Island: A Second Look at the Federal Reserve,*
https://www.amazon.com/Creature-Jekyll-Island-Federal-Reserve/dp/091298645X

49 **"The Next Global Depression is Coming and Optimism Won't Slow It Down,"**
https://time.com/5876606/economic-depression-coronavirus/

50 **Yasko Ishimaru, "Japanese Educational System Problems,"**
https://jhu.sites.tru.ca/files/2019/03/Japanese-Educational-System-Problems.pdf

51 **Klaus Schwab,** *COVID-19: The Great Reset,*
https://www.amazon.com/COVID-19-Great-Reset-Klaus-Schwab/dp/2940631123

52 **"The confidential list of everyone attending the 2020 World Economic Forum in Davos,"**
https://qz.com/1787763/the-list-of-delegates-to-the-2020-world-economic-forum-in-davos/

53 **"A List of CDC Foundation Corporate Donors and Partners Over Time,"**
https://www.cdcfoundation.org/partner-list/corporations

54 **"The confidential list of everyone attending the 2020 World Economic Forum in Davos,"**
https://qz.com/1787763/the-list-of-delegates-to-the-2020-world-economic-forum-in-davos/

55 **"October 2019, Event 201, at the World Economic Forum,"**
https://www.centerforhealthsecurity.org/event201/

56 **"Davos 2021 to be held under theme of The Great Reset,"**
https://www.aa.com.tr/en/economy/davos-2021-to-be-held-under-theme-of-the-great-reset/1863342

SEVEN STEPS TO FREE HOMESCHOOL SUCCESS

57 **"Homeschool Laws by State (U.S.A),"**
https://hslda.org/legal
"Home Education Policies in Europe,"
https://eacea.ec.europa.eu/national-policies/eurydice/sites/default/files/
home_education_in_europe_report.pdf
"Home Education in England: The Facts,"
https://www.theschoolrun.com/home-education-legislation-england

58 **"Transforming the Workforce for Children Birth Through
Age 8: A Unifying Foundation,"** https://www.nap.edu/read/19401/
chapter/8#89

THE EIGHT SECRETS OF HOMESCHOOLED GENIUSES

59 **Robert Waldinger, "Why You Should Listen,"**
https://www.ted.com/speakers/robert_waldinger

60 **"12 Tips For Building Self-Confidence and Self-Belief,"**
https://positivepsychology.com/self-confidence-self-belief/

61 **Peter Wohlleben,** *The Hidden Life of Trees,*
https://www.goodreads.com/book/show/28256439-the-hidden-life-of-trees

62 **Tony Robbins, "The Science of Happiness,"**
https://www.tonyrobbins.com/mental-health/science-of-happiness/

63 **"Learning through Play,"**
https://www.wonderschool.com/p/parent-resources/learning-through-play/

64 **Kira Shaw,** *the Guardian,* **"Travel broadens the mind, but can it
alter the brain?"** https://www.theguardian.com/education/2016/jan/18/
travel-broadens-the-mind-but-can-it-alter-the-brain

65 **Anne Tafton MIT News Office, "How music lessons can
improve language skills,"**
https://news.mit.edu/2018/how-music-lessons-can-improve-language-
skills-0625

66 **Derek Beres, "How reading rewires your brain for higher
intelligence and empathy,"**
https://bigthink.com/high-culture/reading-rewires-your-brain-for-more-
intelligence-and-empathy/

HOW DO HOMESCHOOLED KIDS END UP IN LIFE

67   Susan Peppercorn, "How to Overcome Your Fear of Failure," *Harvard Business Review*, https://hbr.org/2018/12/how-to-overcome-your-fear-of-failure

68   "The Most Empowering Work I Have Done, Which Led Me to Face My Fears Of Failure – Reviews," https://www.landmarkforumnews.com/reviews/

THE FUTURE OF HOMESCHOOLING

69   Rebecca Winthrop, "COVID-19 and school closures," https://www.brookings.edu/research/covid-19-and-school-closures-what-can-countries-learn-from-past-emergencies//

70   "Summer 2020 grades for GCSE, AS and A-level Awards," https://assets.publishing.service.gov.uk/government/uploads/system/uploads/attachment_data/file/908368/Summer_2020_grades_for_GCSE_AS_and_A_level_110820.pdf

71   Philippa Roxby and Nick Triggle, "Scientists not backing Covid jabs for 12 to 15-year-olds," (BBC News), https://www.bbc.com/news/health-58438669

72   "Coronavirus (COVID-19) booster vaccine." Advisory from the U.K. National Health Service, https://www.nhs.uk/conditions/coronavirus-covid-19/coronavirus-vaccination/coronavirus-booster-vaccine/

73   John Hopkins, "Back to School 2021: Helping Kids Get Ready and Stay Safe from Coronavirus," https://www.hopkinsmedicine.org/health/conditions-and-diseases/coronavirus/back-to-school-2021-helping-kids-get-ready-and-stay-safe-from-coronavirus

74   "The Pandemic Caused a Baby Bust, Not a Boom," *Scientific American*, https://www.scientificamerican.com/article/the-pandemic-caused-a-baby-bust-not-a-boom/

75   "Are COVID passports available to minors?" https://www.covidpasscertificate.com/covid-certificates-children-adolescents/

76   "Trends in suicide during the Covid-19 pandemic," https://www.bmj.com/content/371/bmj.m4352

77   "Homeschooling Growing: Multiple Data Points Show Increase 2012 to 2016 and Later," https://www.nheri.org/homeschool-population-size-growing/

78   "Homeschooling Doubled During The Pandemic, U.S. Census Survey Finds," https://www.npr.org/2021/03/22/980149971/homeschooling-doubled-during-the-pandemic-u-s-census-survey-finds

79   N.H.E.R.I., "GENERAL FACTS, STATISTICS, AND TRENDS," https://www.nheri.org/research-facts-on-homeschooling/

80   UNICEF, "Supporting your child's mental health during COVID-19 school returns," https://www.unicef.org/coronavirus/supporting-your-childs-mental-health-during-covid-19-school-return

81   "Homeschooling Experiences and Views During the Pandemic," https://www.edchoice.org/engage/2020-schooling-in-america-series-homeschooling-experiences-and-views-during-the-pandemic/

82   "Strengthening online learning when schools are closed," https://www.oecd.org/coronavirus/policy-responses/strengthening-online-learning-when-schools-are-closed-the-role-of-families-and-teachers-in-supporting-students-during-the-covid-19-crisis-c4ecba6c/

83   "Homeschooling Rates in Vermont, U.S.A. Surge as People Revolt Against Public Indoctrination," https://www.outkick.com/homeschooling-rates-surge-as-people-revolt-against-public-indoctrination/

84   "New Federal Data Confirms Pandemic's Blow to K-12 Enrollment," https://www.the74million.org/article/public-school-enrollment-down-3-percent-worst-century/

85   Betsy De Vos – A brief summary of some of the legal battles she was embroiled in as Education Secretary – focusing on diverting public funding to private educational establishments, https://educationvotes.nea.org/2019/03/22/devos/

86   Josh Eidelson (Bloomberg), "For Teachers Unions, Classroom Reopenings Are the Biggest Test Yet," https://www.bloomberg.com/news/features/2020-10-20/covid-pandemic-classroom-reopenings-are-teachers-unions-biggest-test-yet

87 **"Accelerating Sustainable Development in the 4th Industrial Revolution,"** https://www.pwc.com/gx/en/services/sustainability/publications/accelerating-sustainable-development.html

88 **"The COVID-19 pandemic has changed education forever. This is how,"** https://www.weforum.org/agenda/2020/04/coronavirus-education-global-covid19-online-digital-learning/

89 **N.H.E.R.I., "A Third Reason to Home School: Leadership Development,"** https://www.nheri.org/home-school-researcher-a-third-reason-to-home-school-leadership-development/

90 **H.S.L.D.A., "What Does the Future Hold for Homeschool Freedom?"** https://hslda.org/post/what-does-the-future-hold-for-homeschool-freedom

91 **Klaus Schwab,** *Covid-19: The Great Reset,* https://www.bookdepository.com/Covid-19-Thierry-Malleret/9782940631124

Notes

Notes